Widening the Circle

Widening the Circle

The Power of Inclusive Classrooms

Mara Sapon-Shevin

Beacon Press, Boston

BEACON PRESS
25 Beacon Street
Boston, Massachusetts 02108-2892
www.beacon.org

Beacon Press books
are published under the auspices of
the Unitarian Universalist Association of Congregations.

16 15 14 13 12   12 11 10 9 8

This book is printed on acid-free paper that meets the uncoated paper
ANSI/NISO specifications for permanence as revised in 1992.

Composition by Wilsted & Taylor Publishing Services

Library of Congress Cataloging-in-Publication Data

Sapon-Shevin, Mara.
  Widening the circle : the power of inclusive classrooms / Mara Sapon-Shevin.
    p. cm.
  ISBN-13: 978-0-8070-3280-0 (pbk. : alk. paper)
  ISBN-10: 0-8070-3280-8 (pbk. : alk. paper) 1. Inclusive education—United States.
I. Title.

  LC1201.S28 2007
  371.9'046—dc22   2006025867

"Stand Up" © 2001 by Michael Stern, www.lapointdesign.com/mikesongs, inspired
by the words of Martin Niemoller. "Hey, Little Ant" © 1992 by Phil and Hannah
Hoose. "Walls and Bridges" © 1993, words and music by Sarah Pirtle, Discovery
Center Music, BMI. "That's Not Fair" © 2001, words and music by David Heitler-
Klevans, Two of a Kind. "Courage" © 1990 by Bob Blue, Black Socks Press (BMI).
Reprinted with the permission of Ann Morse and Lara Shepard-Blue.

The writings of Richard Feldman, Jan Boyd, Michael Boyd, Oliver Hersey, Emma
Fialka-Feldman, Micah Fialka-Feldman, and Janice Fialka that are excerpted in the
chapter "Inclusion in Action: Micah's Story," are reprinted with the kind permission of the authors.

For Bob Blue, whose expansive life and fierce commitment to courage continue to transform the world and inspire my heart.

Outwitted

He drew a circle that shut me out
Heretic, rebel, a thing to flout
But Love and I had the wit to win:
We drew a circle that took him in.

Edwin Markham

Contents

Introduction xi

One: Vision

1. Imagining Inclusive Classrooms 3
2. Ten Lessons from Inclusive Classrooms 18

**Two: Challenges: Understanding
and Answering Critics of Inclusion**

3. "What's Wrong with What We're Doing Now?" 63
4. "This Will Be Bad for Everyone" 85
5. "Yes, but You Don't Mean . . ." 108

Interlude: Inclusion in Action: Micah's Story 123

Three: Getting It Right / Doing It Well

6. Building Inclusive Classroom Communities 143
7. Teaching for All and to All 180
8. Taking a Stand for Social Justice 217

Acknowledgments 239

Notes 243

Introduction

We begin with a vision:

Imagine that you are planning a dinner party at your house. What are your hopes and intentions? You want everyone coming to feel welcome and included. You want to provide food that all guests will find appetizing and nourishing. And you want your guests to interact with one another in friendly and congenial ways.

As you think about your party, you think about the guests and who they are. Your friend Robin uses a wheelchair. You'll have to think about accessibility. If you arrange the food buffet-style, will she still have room to get around the table? Your friend Carrie is lactose-intolerant and doesn't eat any dairy products. You'll want to think about the menu so that she'll be sure to have plenty to eat. Your friend Abdullah is Muslim and doesn't eat pork or anything made with lard, and Sharon is on a very low-fat diet. You try to think of what you can serve that will meet everyone's needs.

Some of your guests are very outgoing and will connect easily, but two of your guests, Wynetta and Darrel, are shy and sometimes feel left out. You think about what you can do to make them comfortable, and you hatch some great plans for introducing them to others and asking them both to help with the last-minute salad preparations so that they can have a job and feel engaged during the early stages of the party. Finally, you think about the party itself, and you plan a mixture of time spent in informal getting to know one another and in a short icebreaker that you think will help people to connect and laugh with one another.

Your party is a huge success. Everyone has a great time.

The food is bountiful and well received, and you notice some wonderful connections forming between guests. You reflect back on your planning process and realize that by thinking well about each person who was coming, you were able to design a party that worked well for everyone, meeting individual needs without stigmatizing anyone or isolating him or her from the group. You didn't just make the menu you made last year and then, realizing it wouldn't work for Abdullah, tell him he had better bring his own food. You arranged the physical space so that everyone (including Robin) was able to maneuver around the room, and you didn't leave it to chance that Wynetta would connect well. You also realize that you didn't think about your guests as members of categories: African Americans, vegetarians, physically impaired, socially insecure. You certainly didn't divide your guests into two groups: the "normal" or "regular" ones and the ones with "special needs." Rather, you thought about them as individuals with multiple identities, any of which could contain strengths or embody challenges. And while planning for them as individuals, you were also able to think about them as members of the temporary community you were forming at your house—meeting their needs within a context of commonality and friendship.

WHAT DOES THIS HAVE TO DO WITH SCHOOLS?

This is a book about inclusion and inclusive education—a core value and set of practices that support the belief that all students in a school, regardless of their strengths, weaknesses, or labels—should be full members of the general education school community, with their individual needs met within that general education context. What is at stake, I will argue, is as a way of imagining not only what we want the educational system to look like but what we should want for our children and for the world.

It's within schools that children and adults learn some of the most basic lessons about who matters in the world. This book presents the argument that it is only within inclusive schools that anyone can become a fully loving and competent human being and citizen. And so, I will argue, inclusion is good for—even essential—to a thriving democracy.

This book also argues that inclusion is straightforwardly excellent educational practice that, when implemented thoroughly and conscientiously, can create learning environments that are actively better for all students. Inclusion is as powerful educationally as it is politically. Inclusion is not a favor school systems do for students whom they perceive as "disabled," but a gift to our common humanity—a way of reconceptualizing our schools and our society.

This book describes the many characteristics children bring to schools and classrooms and how the educational system can meet their individual needs within a common, welcoming context. I will explore what our schools could look like if they took inclusion to heart as an organizing principle and value. I will articulate why this matters now, as our nation stands at an educational crossroads deciding what it wants for its children, its schools, and the wider world.

Unlike other books about inclusion and disability, this one will not focus on "categories" of children; you will not find separate sections on how to educate those with cognitive delays, for example, or strategies for organizing instruction for students who are labeled "learning disabled." I will argue, instead, that we must see all children as individuals with multiple identities and design curricula and instruction that is responsive to many aspects of a child's life. I will explore strategies that cross "categories" of children, showing that good inclusion is good teaching. And I will discuss ways of creating accepting, open, humane classrooms that welcome all children and that meet their individual needs within a context of shared community.

It is important that schools do inclusion well—and that doesn't mean throwing diverse students together with little planning, support, or resources. I hope to convince you that if we create quality inclusive schools, we will have better children, better teachers, better curriculum, better pedagogy, and a better collective future.

THE VISION

To many people, the word "inclusion" is associated primarily or exclusively with the practice of including students with disabilities in regular classrooms. Although this is certainly one definition, it is a limited one, and one that often solidifies differences in ways that are counterproductive. The truth, however, is that all children come to school with a wide range of characteristics and that every child has multiple identities, all of which affect his/her school experience and achievement.

In the first section of this book, I explore a vision of inclusion that goes far beyond issues of disability and special education, although it includes them. I argue that an inclusive school is one which attends thoughtfully and well to all the differences that students bring with them to school. These include differences in race, ethnicity, language, family composition, gender, religion, sexual orientation, dis/ability, socioeconomic status, and so on. Teachers must pay as much attention to a child's race, family background, home language, religion, and interests as to an overarching label the child has been given, such as "retarded" or "gifted." And we must also not pay so much attention to differences that we forget the powerful human similarities that cross all boundaries.

THE CHALLENGES

There have been many challenges and objections to the concept and implementation of inclusion in schools. Some of these have been practical (space, time, training, resources), and some have been more basic—inclusion has been dismissed as a bad idea that conflicts with the essential goals of schooling. Often, the practical and logistical complexities are raised as a smoke screen for more deeply held beliefs about human diversity, equity, social justice, and relationships. By exploring the ways in which inclusion has been challenged, we can explore underlying beliefs about education and democratic schooling that manifest themselves in current school practices and debates.

This section of the book addresses these challenges head-on, responds to the most commonly raised *yes, buts* about inclusion and inclusive schools—from parents, teachers, school leaders and policy makers—and explores myths and beliefs that impede inclusion and inclusive practices.

GETTING IT RIGHT/DOING IT WELL

In many situations, inclusion has failed because teachers, administrators, parents, and students have been underprepared and inadequately supported. Simply dumping students in regular classrooms without addressing issues of exclusion, teasing, curriculum modification, peer support, and pedagogical differentiation dooms inclusion to failure. It is critical to differentiate between a good idea badly implemented and a bad idea. It has been said that there is no good way to do the wrong thing. But it is also true that the right thing done poorly or thoughtlessly is unlikely to be successful.

This section provides practical examples and strategies for making inclusion successful. It addresses issues of dealing with diversity, curriculum, pedagogy, and classroom climate. It describes how we can create classrooms and schools that are consistent with our vision.

Inclusive education is an idea that has gained incredible visibility in the last twenty years; there are journals of inclusive education, conferences devoted to inclusion, inclusive education teacher education programs, and textbooks and articles that address inclusive practices. Many schools explicitly name inclusion as part of their mission statement, and litigation regarding educational practice has forced many districts to increase the extent to which they serve students with disabilities in the general education environment. It is unlikely that inclusion—as a concept or a practice—will go away. It is not simply an educational reform but an entirely different way of conceptualizing educational practice.

At the same time, there have been numerous challenges to the principles and practice of inclusion. Many schools have racially resegregated, and some school districts have pulled back from their commitment to integrating students of different racial groups and abilities; charter schools and proposals for privatization threaten the very notion of democratic schooling and the implementation of inclusive practices. With so much hanging in the balance, we cannot wait any longer to embrace a commitment to inclusion. The book concludes with an exploration of the urgency for making our schools inclusive in order to ensure—and I don't believe I am overstating this—the survival of a democratic society. Part Three allows us to explore real schools and real classrooms that have implemented inclusive practice—chances to see inclusion in action and to understand that the vision of inclusive education is within our grasp and worthy of our dedication.

One: Vision

1. Imagining Inclusive Classrooms

Contrast the following two situations:

John, a quiet twelve-year-old sixth grader at your local middle school, goes through the cafeteria lunch line at noon. After he pays for his food and drink, he goes to put his tray down at a table already occupied by other students. One of the boys at the table tells him to go away. John leaves the table and approaches the students at another table. There he is told, "Get out of here." John walks away and puts his tray down at a third table, realizes he's forgotten his straw, and goes back to the lunch line to get one. When he returns to the table where he left his lunch, he finds his tray gone.

Maria, a fourth grader, has recently moved to the United States from Mexico. Her English is limited, and she is extremely shy. The teacher and students initiate Spanish lessons for the whole class, with Maria at the center as a co-teacher. They decide to begin every day with two songs, one in Spanish and one in English, so that they can share music and language. The children become vigilant about making sure Maria learns playground games and is included in their activities. When she is teased on the playground, they quickly intercede and support her.

What do these scenarios say about schools? And what do they say about what children are learning? More important, what kinds of adults and citizens will the children in these two scenarios become? What kinds of people do we want to populate our world?

Perhaps you are familiar with a term that began to be used in the late 1970s after the passage of PL 94-142 (The Education of All Handicapped Children Act). The word "mainstreaming" (although not used in the law) became the common term for the practice of placing students with disabilities in regular

3

classrooms with their chronological peers for certain classes, activities, or portions of the day. Special education teachers, in consultation with other school personnel, typically decided when a child was deemed ready to be mainstreamed, and then the child was allowed to go to a regular class.

There were many problems with this model, some of which I experienced personally when I taught special education. To begin with, the separation of regular education teachers and special education teachers (different schedules, different preparation periods, different school duties) meant that it was often difficult for special education teachers and regular education teachers to form the kind of relationship necessary for optimal collaboration and problem solving. As a special education teacher, I had very little idea what went on in the regular third grade, so it was hard to know when and how one of my students, Michael, could be successfully included. Being out of touch with what typical children were like, it was also too easy to see any of Michael's imperfect behavior as indicative of his lack of readiness, rather than knowing that all children are imperfect some of the time!

I will never forget the teacher who once said to me about a student with a history of behavioral problems: "Kevin's behavior has gotten much better, but I don't think he's quite ready to go back to the sixth grade quite yet, because about once a week he still swears." My response was, "Hell, he'll do fine!" In many classrooms, a sixth-grade boy who swore once a week would be unremarkable. In the context of segregated classrooms, when we define ourselves as special educators and become so accustomed to thinking about behavior in terms of deviance and problems, the kind of variation in behavior and compliance to norms that *all* children exhibit becomes a reason to continue the segregation of some kids. We forget about how much human variation we are surrounded by all the time when we focus on who and what is "normal." In considering whether to mainstream Michael, I had to judge whether he would be able to participate fully without specific supports or accommodations, and I was reluctant to send him out of my "safe" space when I had little idea what he would encounter. Many parents of students with disabilities were also reluctant to send their children to the regular classroom when they had been told by school officials (sometimes not that long before) that it was only in the special classroom that their children's needs could be met. Many parents were fearful of returning their child (who perhaps was finally experiencing some success) to the very setting that had excluded him or labeled her as uneducable or deficient.

A phrase found in much of the educational literature of that time illuminates some of these problems. The general guideline offered for determining the right time to "mainstream" a child was this: "The child should be mainstreamed when he/she can compete in the regular classroom." Several aspects of this statement are problematic. First, it assumes that the regular classroom will inevitably be structured competitively and that the child with disabilities will therefore be expected to behave competitively to be successful. Since competitive models, by definition, create winners and losers, it wasn't difficult to see that the child in question—usually a child with a history of school failure or significant challenges—was likely to be the loser in this situation.

Second, the statement presupposes that it is the job of the child to fit into the existing classroom structure: this is how we do things here; if it works for you, great, and if not, well I guess you weren't ready. Little or no burden or responsibility is placed on the teacher and students in the regular classroom to modify what they do to create a successful learning environment for the mainstreamed child (or for anyone else).

Inclusion, by contrast, is a model that begins with the right of every child to be in the mainstream of education. Students do not have to "earn" their way into the classroom with their behavior or skills. They are assumed to be full members—perhaps with modifications, adaptations, and extensive support—but they are members nonetheless. Rather than saying, "This is my classroom—let's see if you can fit in," inclusion asks teachers to think about all aspects of their classroom—pedagogy, curriculum, and classroom climate—in order to make the environment educative and welcoming for all students. It is a mutual process of adaptation and accommodation, with the goal being full inclusion with supports.

As a metaphor, consider the game of musical chairs, in which children walk around chairs to the music and then, when the music stops, must grab a chair to win. In the typical game of musical chairs, the child who is different—slower, smaller, doesn't speak English, didn't understand the rules—is eliminated almost immediately. What is the message about difference? Roughly speaking, we learn: if you're different, you lose.

The other players have no obligation to the student who is struggling, and their success does not in any way depend on helping that student to be successful. This is a mainstreaming model. It says, When you can play this game with us successfully, you are welcome to join.

Inclusion asks a different set of questions. Inclusion asks: How can the game be modified so that everyone can play? How can the game be structured so that all players help one another? Inclusion can best be understood by the radically different game of *cooperative* musical chairs, in which everybody plays and everybody wins. All the children remain in the game from the start to the finish. What changes—as the number of chairs decreases—are the problem-solving configurations necessary to keep everyone involved.

This is how the game works: Children walk around chairs to the music, and then, when the music stops, all children must be on a chair for the group to win. The game begins without too much challenge; there are ten students who must fit themselves onto nine chairs. With a little bit of chair-sharing, the children can make it work; Mona shares a chair with Shay. But then, the game gets more difficult as, one by one, chairs are withdrawn; ten children must figure out how to fit themselves onto eight chairs—and they must all be on a chair for the round to be a success. Students have to watch one another carefully to assess who needs help and support. Littler children must be accommodated on laps, children who don't understand the game—perhaps because they have never played or because they aren't familiar with the game's terminology—must be assisted so they can participate. After each successful round, a chair is removed, and soon ten children are figuring out how to manage on seven chairs, then on six, and so on. The group does not *win* unless every child is part of the group supported on chairs. There is great joy when ten children figure out how to make themselves fit on three chairs, and often there is laughter and giggling as unsupported body parts are identified and incorporated into the heap!

This is an inclusion model; we acknowledge the challenges, and we figure out—together—how to make it work. We don't abandon people who are having trouble. We don't celebrate "I won" unaware or indifferent to those who are struggling. We don't ask children to fit into an existing, fiercely competitive activity. Rather, we change the game so that it is fun and accessible for everyone. And we structure the game to promote interdependence and support. Parenthetically, I must add that cooperative musical chairs is actually much *more* challenging than the traditional version. It requires intense problem solving and communication, trial-and-error tests of solutions, and a subsequent assessment of strategies. When compared to the skills necessary to "win" regular musical chairs—pushing and shoving—it becomes clear which game is harder and which is better preparation for living together in community.

WHAT INCLUSION IS NOT

There is no question that in some classrooms, schools and districts, the rhetoric of inclusion has been used to justify eliminating services and unceremoniously "dumping" students with significant educational needs back into the mainstream with little or no preparation or support. If this is what you have seen, it's not surprising that the concept of inclusion seems ill-founded and bound to fail. But it is important not to reject a concept and commitment because of poor, half-hearted implementation. Holding those who espouse the goal of inclusion to high standards is a critical part of making inclusion successful.

Parallels can be drawn with other attempts at integration that bring together groups who have been historically separated. In Cleveland, Ohio, for example, court-ordered racial desegregation was initiated on Monday, September 10, 1979. I was living in Cleveland at the time and remember reading a news story that told that one of the participating white schools placed all the incoming black students in a separate classroom on a different floor. This, the schools believed, met the "letter of the law" because the students were attending the same school. Then they communicated vociferously that desegregation didn't work because none of the students had developed interracial relationships, and the achievement disparity between white and black students remained constant. It seems disingenuous to say that "desegregation doesn't work"—to reject a complex concept that demands systemic and structural changes—when the implementation was so limited and half-hearted. A more accurate statement would be "attempts at desegregation implemented without thoughtful planning and consistent monitoring are unlikely to succeed." The same can be said about inclusion.

Another key concept of inclusion, properly understood, is that students with disabilities should be represented in the school in "natural proportions." That is, if children with disabilities represent 10 percent of the overall student population, then no classroom or school should have more than 10 percent of their students be children with such challenges. Unfortunately, this is not the way inclusion policies usually play out in schools, for several reasons. At the most basic level, when principals or district administrators are deciding where to place students with challenges, they look for welcoming, accommodating schools and teachers, whose curricular and pedagogical practices support diversity and inclusion. Sadly, this has often meant that schools and teachers who meet these criteria receive *all* of the students with disabilities, and those that are rigid, unwelcoming, or reluctant do not receive any. This invariably results in uneven distributions, often followed by resentment and grumbling. "Good" teachers often burn out because they have been given more challenging classes, and teachers who have stated their unwillingness to accommodate students with significant differences are allowed to continue to use rigid and unwelcoming models in their classrooms. Similarly, welcoming schools can quickly be positioned to serve disproportionate numbers of students with disabilities.

At another structural level, patterns of staffing and supplying support services often result in the creation of "inclusion classrooms" that serve many more students with significant challenges than would be predicted by the principle of natural proportions. A classroom, for example, with twelve students with Individual Education Programs (descriptive educational plans for students' support and services) and twelve "typical" students tends to resemble a special education classroom much more than it does a typical classroom, eliminating many of the goals and benefits (as we will see) of an inclusion model. The use of the term "the inclusion classroom" should make us wonder: if Mrs. Robert's third-grade class is "the inclusion third grade," then what is Mr. Willet's room next door—the exclusion third grade? If only a small number of classrooms are singled out to forward the mission of inclusion, it signals a larger failure to commit to inclusion in the sense that I mean to advocate.

WHY INCLUSION IS NOT JUST ABOUT DISABILITY ISSUES

An inclusive definition of inclusion goes far beyond students with disabilities and looks at the myriad ways that students differ from one another: race, class, gender, ethnicity, family background, sexual orientation, language, abilities, size, religion, and on and on. Unless teachers have thirty cloned children, there is—and always has been—considerable diversity. Inclusion as a school policy didn't create the differences in our classrooms, but inclusion does allow teachers to name the diversity, value it, and strategize about productive and sensitive responses. The opposite of an inclusive classroom is one that is still (inevitably) heterogeneous, but that makes the differences in the classroom invisible to us and others and asks professionals to teach in some standard way while *pretending* to be responsive. Inclusion demands that we not be surprised or distressed by the differences in our classroom but rather embrace these as both inevitable and desirable.

The differences schools must think about are numerous, since everyone has multiple identities, including racial, ethnic, religious, familial, language, gender, and so on. Inclusive schooling requires that teachers be responsive to the whole child, and not simply to one aspect or characteristic. Adapting a Christmas craft activity for Joshua, who has cerebral palsy and uses a communication board, may not be an appropriate or adequate response to his individual identity when Joshua is Jewish and does not celebrate Christmas. If Joshua is defined according to only one dimension of his identity, it is hard to meet his needs and treat him with respect. A better, more inclusive solution would be to have all children participate in a craft activity that is not linked to a particular holiday and that allows for multiple ways to conceptualize and complete the task. When the activity is making fish or other underwater creatures for a class bulletin board on the ocean, for example, there are ways for children of all artistic abilities and motor-behavior levels to contribute.

The books in the book corner and the stories read should represent all families. Rather than limiting available reading materials to books that portray only European American, two-parent families, schools should create classrooms in which all children see themselves reflected—and validated—

by the curriculum and classroom practices. This need not be done self-consciously ("Now, children, we're going to read a book about a family that's really different. . . .") but simply as part of what goes on in class. Why shouldn't *all* children hear books about Hanukah, Kwanzaa, and Ramadan? Books in which families come in many variations of number and membership? Books in which characters live, work, play, and interact in a variety of languages? Doing so enriches all listeners.

Attending to multiple identities and needs can feel overwhelming, but the good news is that being thoughtful and responsive to one issue does not make us less responsive or thoughtful about another. In fact, the nature of good teaching is that it is universal; when the social environment is welcoming and accepting of children with disabilities, establishing norms of acceptance and inclusion, this also improves the classroom atmosphere for students who are overweight, come from different family backgrounds, or eat foods that classmates may find "different." A reading program that allows all children to access literature that is appropriate to their reading level and their interests enriches the literacy environment for children of all reading abilities, for those who access print through computer-assisted instruction, and for those whose primary language is other than English. Many teachers report that an accommodation or modification that they originally made for one student turned out to be appropriate or helpful for other students. In one school, the students identified as "learning disabled" were taught to take notes using a T-chart. Then teachers discovered that *most* students could benefit from this strategy. In an elementary classroom, a teacher made a daily schedule for a child who always wanted to know

"What comes next?"—and found out that many students felt more grounded and focused when they knew the order of their day. A "circle of friends" (a friendship strategy) constructed for a child who was isolated revealed that many other students didn't have friends or anyone to play with on weekends, and so the strategy was extended to include the whole class. When we no longer think of students as "the same" and "different," then we are able to make changes that support multiple forms of heterogeneity within a common context of community.

Not only does inclusive education require attention to all differences (race, language, religion, family background, dis/ability, etc.) but also to the whole school and every part of the day. Can nonacademic experiences include a wide variety of students? Is participation in the school play only a possibility for students who are physically able and verbally adept, or are there many ways to be part of the play? When educator and children's musician Bob Blue was producing a children's play of *Alice in Wonderland,* he was able to maximize the number and kinds of children who participated. Rather than choosing one child to be Alice (and disappointing the other six girls who wanted the role), he cast seven Alices, and each scene had a different Alice—whoever was wearing the blue dress was Alice. A student who was able to speak only through a touch-activated communication device was the narrator and pushed the appropriate button when it was his turn. Students who were shy or reluctant to be on stage had backstage jobs and were also given the opportunity to change their minds about taking a speaking role. As the rehearsals went on, some children who had initially been adamant about their nonparticipation changed their minds and took places on the stage.

What does it mean to think inclusively? A few examples may help us to understand that inclusion is as much intention and commitment as it is a particular model or set of strategies.

• Inclusion means asking about access: "Will everyone be able to go on the field trip?" It means understanding that access is a complex issue and that we have to think about everyone in our group. If the museum isn't accessible to a person in our group who uses a wheelchair, then we will figure out a solution, or we won't go. We won't tell Marie that we're going without her and that we'll tell her about it when we return. If the field trip is scheduled on an important Islamic holiday, so that four members of our group will miss it, it's not a numerical issue ("Well, most of the class can go on that date") but a matter of principle, and the trip is rescheduled. If someone in our group doesn't speak English, how do we make the museum guide's speech accessible and meaningful? And if several students in the class can't afford the trip, teachers either raise money for it or find a field trip that isn't as expensive. We don't leave some students behind.

• Inclusion means asking about cultures and beliefs: What snack can everyone eat? How can birthdays be celebrated when some class members aren't allowed to participate in parties? Inclusion means knowing enough about one another to plan a snack or a meal that allows everyone to participate. It's not about choosing a steakhouse for dinner because some people like steak and leaving the vegetarians behind. It's a commitment to learning enough about one another so that we can make meaningful choices and can problem solve so that people aren't left out or marginalized.

• Inclusion means generating strategies so that everyone who wants to have someone to eat with at lunch has someone! It's not about cliques and secret alliances that exclude; it's not about being oblivious to the person who is alone or lonely; it's not about me. It's about us. And it doesn't matter why someone is alone, or even whether they "deserve" to be alone because they're "different" or annoying or irritating. It's about figuring out how to connect and how to support one another so that everyone can participate.

• Inclusion means valuing multiple forms of communication for everyone. We teach some sign language to all the children, enriching their lives and perspectives as well as allowing them to communicate with a child who is hearing impaired. Even a first grader who is able to sign only "Hello, my name is Dana" is much less likely to tease or be fearful of people who are deaf or hearing impaired. We all learn some Spanish so that we can increase the number of people we can talk to and cultures we can learn about, and in the process we learn that not speaking English doesn't imply anything about a person's intelligence or worth. When one child in the class needs to increase his arm strength and flexibility, all children practice yoga and stretching exercises so that they all get stronger and more flexible.

• Inclusion is about structuring our classrooms so that typical hierarchies of "smartness" are broken down and replaced with an understanding that there are many ways to be smart. Inclusion is about a classroom in which a visitor asking, "Who's the smartest child in here?" would be met with blank stares or by a detailed answer: "Well, Justin is really great at drawing pictures; Manolita is an amazing dancer and really knows how to move; Jazon is so good at chess, it's amazing; and Deneva remembers everything she's ever read and can tell you about the story," and so on.

Most important, inclusion means engaging all members of the school community in explicit discussions of the value of inclusiveness. These conversations are sometimes easier with children than with adults, many of whom have been socialized to accept meritocracy and elitism as natural and inevitable. Children have an innate sense of fairness and justice. Their willingness to assert "That's not fair" and their careful scrutiny of others' behavior and resources is linked to their understandings of what fairness means and can be used to good advantage in engaging them in discussions of the differences between "same" and "fair," for example, or in understanding more complex notions of accommodation and differentiation.

I had a conversation with third graders in a school that was considering a move from heterogeneous classes to homogeneous, tracked classrooms at each grade level. I asked their opinion: "What do you think about the idea of having three fourth grades—one for the kids who are really smart, one for the kids who are medium, and one for the kids who aren't as smart?" Their response was immediate: "That's a really bad idea!" "Why?" I asked. "Because," said one girl, "first of all, it would really hurt kids' feelings." "And," added another girl, "who would help the kids who needed help if you put all the kids who knew more in different classes?" A third child added, "Yeah, and besides, who would decide who was smart and who wasn't. I mean, like smart at what?"

These third graders did not need to read the professional research literature on tracking, peer tutoring, self-esteem, and self-fulfilling prophecy, although all of these support the benefits of inclusion. They realized, from their own experience, that separating children according to some putative set of characteristics was highly problematic. They understood that there were many ways to be smart, they valued the ways in which they had helped one another to learn, and they understood that there were affective components to education as well as academic goals.

These are big lessons. What lessons do we want for our children? What are we teaching? What world will we create by the education we provide?

2. Ten Lessons from Inclusive Classrooms

I believe that there are ten lessons to be learned from inclusive education and that some of these can be learned only in this setting. These are all lessons that speak directly to the qualities and skills we need in all our children and in all our citizens. By exploring these ten lessons, we can begin to understand why inclusion matters and how the ways we structure schools and classrooms affect not only the quality of our children's education but their abilities to shape their world in the future.

UNDERSTANDING DIFFERENCE

It seems obvious to say that we can understand and value differences only if we are surrounded by them. Otherwise, our understanding, our acceptance, and even our tolerance is an academic issue.

Within inclusive settings, students are not only exposed to a vast array of people and their differences, but also learn how to talk about these differences, to ask thoughtful questions, to connect. Many adults are remarkably awkward about differences in race, religion, ethnicity, appearance, and so on. My white university students consistently stumble when trying to talk about racial differences. "Should I say 'black' or 'African American' or what? If someone is from Jamaica or Haiti, are they still called African American?" Lack of experience with difference coupled with limited conversations about how to *have* the conversation leave us uncomfortable and awkward.

When I first met my friend Robin, who uses a wheelchair,

18

I was clumsy and apprehensive. Since I was a professor of inclusive education, I knew that I was supposed to be accepting and comfortable and that I was expected to know what to do (open the door, help or not help, mention or not mention her disabilities, etc.). But the truth is that I, having grown up in largely segregated settings, had never been friends with someone with a physical disability. I wanted to "do the right thing," but I simply didn't know what that was.

Fifteen years later, Robin is one of my closest friends. I have learned through experience and her patient teaching how to help her put her jacket on, how to put things back in her backpack in just the right place so she can find them, and how to push her wheelchair so as to negotiate curbs and ramps with grace. We've had funny moments when I tried to help and got it all wrong, and aggravating moments when we've discovered the handicapped parking space occupied by people who didn't seem to need it. I've watched her be treated thoughtfully and respectfully, and I've witnessed waitresses asking *me* what Robin would like to eat. I have also learned that most of our relationship isn't about her disability, but about a shared love of music, humor, Judaism, and peace activism. I've learned that Robin is an attentive listener, an honest critic, and a wonderful friend.

But I came to this relationship with a significant disability, one that was, in many ways, far more significant than Robin's. My disability was a profound lack of knowledge and comfort with disabilities. As a product of my schooling and my lack of experience, I was limited in my understanding, and my nervousness was a reflection of knowing that I didn't know what to do.

Children who grow up in inclusive schools learn to be comfortable and knowledgeable about many differences. My own daughter Leora, who attended an elementary school famous for its focus on inclusive education, was, at age nine, completely relaxed with people with cerebral palsy, people who used communication devices, and people whose behavior was quite different from her own.

When we moved to Syracuse, New York, Leora began attending Ed Smith Elementary School, where she was a classmate to students with a range of abilities/disabilities, many of whom used alternative communication devices. Shortly after we arrived there, we had a visit from Robert Williams, who was then the commissioner of the Administration on Developmental Disabilities (and became the director of the Office on Disability, Aging, and Long Term Care Policy under the Clinton administration) and his partner, Helen. Bob, a gifted advocate and writer, has cerebral palsy and, because speaking is challenging for him, sometimes uses an electronic speech machine. During his visit, we went out to dinner at a local family-style restaurant. Eight of us sat around the table, including Bob, Helen, Leora, and me. The young waitress approached Bob and asked him what he wanted. He made some vocalizations that weren't easily understandable and then typed into his communication device (which then spoke for him) that he wanted lemonade with his dinner. The waitress did a reasonable job of attending to his communication and his requests. Leora, meanwhile, was watching the interaction with great intensity. She was vigilant as Bob's ally and eager to see how this young woman would deal with him. The waitress then approached Bob's partner, Helen, and whispered, "What's wrong with him?" As soon as the waitress had left, Leora was out of her chair like a shot, asking Helen, "What did she say?" Helen repeated the waitress's comment. Leora shook her head ruefully, "Gee, you'd think she'd never seen a communication device before." We chuckled and explained to Leora that probably the waitress never *had* seen such a machine. What was "ordinary" and "unremarkable" to Leora was not within the experience and comfort level of the young waitress.

This is one of the gifts of inclusion. Inclusion allows our children to grow up knowledgeable about things that even we, as adults, find challenging or uncomfortable. But we must be incredibly vigilant about what lessons our children are learning about difference. Just as people have become much more aware of how people of color are represented in the media, so we must be aware of how disability is represented to those who are "learning the culture."

When Leora was fifteen, she took a driver's education course at a local high school. Unfortunately, the course focused more on scaring the students than on teaching them to drive. The class took four field trips: one to a graveyard, one to an emergency room, one to traffic court, and one to an automobile junkyard. And, in addition to this, each week the students viewed a movie designed to frighten them into being good drivers. With each successive class, Leora came home increasingly upset; they saw movies of mothers crying at their dead children's grave sites, people flying through windshields and breaking bones, bloody wrecks on the highway, and so on. Though I am willing to concede that there *may* have been a student in the class who already knew how to drive and needed to learn more caution, clearly, this was the wrong curriculum for my child, who didn't know how to drive and was already very nervous about driving.

The last night of class, my daughter came home very shaken. She described in detail the movie they had seen that night. The film told the story of a young teenage woman who had been in a drunken-driving accident during her high school years. Speaking from her wheelchair, she described her accident and what her life had been like since she became paralyzed. The young woman's closing lines were: "I used to go out with my friends on the weekends, now I stay at home. I used to have a future to look forward to, now there's nothing to look forward to. I used to have a life, now I have nothing."

Leora told me this story with great agitation and then said, plaintively, "Mama, I know the movie was supposed to be about drunk driving, but all I could think about was what you taught me about inclusion. And I kept wondering, 'Why doesn't she have friends, why doesn't she have a future, why doesn't she have a life?' "

If these are the images our children (and we) see about disability, it is small wonder that the prospect of inclusive classrooms in which we would interact regularly with people with disabilities sounds depressing and grim. What we teach people about human variation as children will have a profound effect on their understanding of difference in the future and their abilities to connect to and relate to people who are different from them.

Inclusion allows us to acknowledge that the traditional categories of "able bodied" and "disabled" don't make much sense because we are all complex humans, and the line between "us" and "them" is constantly shifting and therefore meaningless. When we construct a duality of normal/abnormal, usually with ourselves on the "normal" side and other people labeled as "abnormal," we not only limit our connections and relationships with those whom we perceive as "other," but we also impede our ability to know ourselves as multifaceted people with strengths, challenges, and peculiarities.

In the book *The Curious Incident of the Dog in the Nighttime*, by Mark Haddon, the narrator, a young man with a form of autism, talks about his reliance and appreciation of time schedules. He maps out his day carefully: 7:40 A.M., breakfast; 8 A.M., put clothes on; 8:05 A.M., pack school bag; and so on. He says that the weekends are challenging for him because the time schedule is different, and his trip to France even more challenging because there was no appreciable timetable. Is this proclivity for a timetable, this need for order and regularity, this preference for predictability a symptom of autism, or is it part of the personalities and preferences of a significant portion of the population? Labeling this behavior as part of a disability or pathologizing it does a disservice to all of us who maintain schedules and lists and timetables, and it keeps us from seeing the many ways that we are the same as those who acquire labels for their behavior.

Teachers in inclusive settings typically report that having a child with a more significant "difference" in the class forces an interrogation of many kinds of diversity and important discussions about how we want our differences discussed and responded to. Are Michael, who requires tube feeding, and Noah, who is a vegetarian, and Ranit, who has numerous food allergies, that different in terms of wanting their particular needs to be respected and accommodated in the classroom community? Is refraining from making fun of Carlos because of his stutter that different from dealing kindly with Lauren, who reads haltingly, or Corey, who often bumps into people when he crosses the room?

One first-grade teacher, reporting on her challenging and

powerful learning experiences in having Martha, a seven-year-old with Down syndrome, in her class, said, "It taught us all that it's okay to be different." She said she knew that the lessons had stuck when Jack, one of her "typical" first graders, responded to an older child who dismissed Jack's library book as a "baby book." Jack, nonplussed, said, "I guess we all read different books!"

Inclusive classrooms teach us that we are all different and that we want to be talked about respectfully. The language we use—and the labels—are profoundly important in shaping our own understanding and others' perceptions. Calling me a "middle-aged, organizationally challenged woman" feels very different from calling me "a creative woman in her prime who grasps the big picture rather than being mired in petty details." Both descriptions are true, but which one would make you think, "Gee, I'd like to hang out with that woman!"? What we call people does matter, and inclusive settings help us to expand our vocabularies, widen our lens, and sharpen our kindness skills.

What is at stake here is big. It is through our relationships with others, particularly those whom we perceive as "different" from us, that we learn who we are. We learn how to treat others, and we begin to articulate how we want to be treated as well. We learn to care for others or to turn away from their pain. We learn to reach out or to withdraw. We learn that it's "each person for him/herself," or we learn that we are a community, interconnected and interdependent.

PERSPECTIVE TAKING

Being with people who differ in many ways—surrounding ourselves with those who are challenged by situations in which we feel at ease or who are comfortable in situations in which we feel stretched—teaches us important lessons in perspective-taking as well.

We learn that not everyone experiences the world the way we do. As anthropologist and ethnobotanist Wade Davis says, "The world in which you were born is just one model of reality. Other cultures are not failed attempts at being you. They are unique manifestations of the human spirit."

People who are different from us—whose differences we acknowledge and understand—help us to realize that we aren't the center of the universe and that other people's experiences are equally valid. This ability to see the world through someone else's lens greatly expands our ability to navigate in an increasingly complex world and to do so with skill and grace.

I was lucky to have lived abroad as a young child. I attended first grade in Spain and second grade in Scotland. By the time I returned to the United States for third grade, I was a changed person. I knew that there were many different kinds of food in the world, that people spoke lots of different languages (some of which I understood, and many of which I didn't), I knew that people wore different clothing (in Scotland, men wore kilts and knee socks), and I realized that there were many ways to be in the world. When other children would tell me, "You can't eat that for breakfast," or "That's not how you're supposed to do that," I already knew that there were more possibilities and that knowing more options made my life richer and my future possibilities broader.

Understanding others' lives also helps us become clearer about our own beliefs and values. In a culture that values individualism and privacy, for example, it is helpful to know that these principles are not universally held. The day after a

Hmong child in Minneapolis stayed at the home of her Caucasian, American classmate, she told her teacher: "It's so sad! Their house is so big, they each have to sleep in their own room!" Rather than understanding that a five-bedroom house for a family of four was a symbol of affluence and success, this girl viewed it as lonely and unfortunate. Her own perspective—that sharing a room with her sisters was a desirable, loving, and comforting opportunity—clearly bumped up against another set of beliefs, and hearing her reactions allows us to think seriously about our own assumptions.

One often hears stories about life-altering experiences that help people to reformulate their values and priorities. A man nearly dies of a heart attack and subsequently rethinks his life's priorities; a family loses everything in a flood and establishes a new appreciation of people rather than possessions. For me, the lesson came ten years ago in a hospital in Australia. My whole family had gone with me to Australia, where I taught and lectured on inclusion, community building, and friendship. Halfway through our time there, my daughter Dalia, then fifteen, was bitten by an insect in the rainforest and came down with a rare tropical disease. Through a series of misdiagnoses and inappropriate prescriptions (we were told she had the flu and to give her acetaminophen), Dalia ended up in a coma with liver failure, kidney failure, and respiratory arrest. For nearly ten days, she lay in intensive care in a coma, connected to a variety of life-support machines. The doctors were not encouraging about her survival, given the number of vital organs affected; they told us that she had a 5 percent chance to live. It was the most terrifying experience of my life. It seemed incomprehensible that in a two-day period we had gone from being a family on a trip to a family with a child dying in intensive care.

After ten agonizing days, through a combination of superb medical care, enormous amounts of prayer and support from every corner of the earth, and a feisty and resilient child, Dalia emerged from her coma. She began breathing again, eating, and finally walking. She made a full recovery.

I learned many lessons from this experience—from Dalia's survival and the support we all received—but one of the most profound was a lesson in *what really matters*. I know many people who are troubled by teenagers; they don't like their music, their clothes, their hair colors, or their tattoos. But as I watched my child in a coma, it became very clear to me that none of those things really mattered. The only thing that I wanted was for my child to live, to begin breathing again on her own, with her kidneys, lungs, and liver functioning. Sitting by her bedside, watching various machines breathing for my daughter, monitoring her heart and keep her alive, I said to her, "Dalia, if you just get better, you can have purple hair!" (this had been a sticking point between us earlier).

When Dalia emerged from her coma, I not only "allowed" the purple hair, I bought the hair dye for her myself! My sense of perspective was profoundly altered in a way that has stayed with me since then and will (I hope) forever.

One of my most powerful experiences about disability—and how others view it—came in the slow recovery period after Dalia was released from the hospital. Because of the severity of her illness, we needed to stay in Australia for her to get her strength back. Staying in a little apartment near the hospital, we concentrated on getting Dalia to eat and regain her strength. About a week after Dalia's release from the hospital—all of us a bit stir crazy—we had the incredible pleasure of going to an outdoor art festival. An Australian friend picked us up—Dalia in her wheelchair—and we headed out for our first "family outing" in almost a month. We were ecstatic. The day was sunny, and, as we pushed Dalia in her wheelchair, we noticed every little thing with joy. Our child was alive, we were together, and all was well. Then, we all noticed (Dalia included) that people were staring at us as a family—father, mother, and two daughters, one in a wheelchair. And their looks were unmistakably those of concern, sympathy, and, yes, pity. We heard little *tsk-tsk* noises, and the murmurs of "Oh, how sad, that sweet girl is in a wheelchair."

And we howled with laughter!

It was funny, ridiculous, ironic, and silly to us that we, so full of great joy and tremendous relief, were for others objects of pity! Dalia turned to me and whispered, "Mama, they feel sorry for me!"

I realized in that moment that we make judgments about one another's lives—and particularly about those with disabilities—that are ill-founded and, sometimes, just plain wrong! We assume that there is nothing but sadness and grief in the lives of people with disabilities and their parents and families. We feel pity, we feel fear, and we feel discomfort. None of those feelings encourage us to seek relationships or get closer. We miss the moments of joy and tenderness, of love and success. Noticing more of *those* moments would lead us to connection and comfort.

I will never forget the father whom I met at a workshop for parents of children with disabilities. He told me a story that points to our limited understanding and vision—and the potential damage of our unexamined assumptions. His son had been born with significant disabilities and had nearly died at birth. Shortly after his birth, a social worker had come to meet with the family to talk about their situation. Although clearly concerned about their child's future and challenges, the parents were nonetheless thrilled that their son was doing as well as he was, and they were full of plans for his future and their life as a family.

The social worker must have felt that, somehow, the parents were not grieving sufficiently, or were in some stage of denial, because she kept insisting how dire the situation was and how grim the child's life would be. Finally, in a moment of exasperation, she turned to the parents and said: "Let me explain it to you this way. Your son will never do anything you'll be proud of."

With tears in his eyes, the father said to me, "My son didn't learn to walk until he was almost three, and when I saw how hard he tried and how much he struggled, I was never prouder of anyone in my whole life. I will never forgive that woman for telling me that about my son."

When we are surrounded by a broader range of the human condition, it helps us to remember what it important. It reshapes our perspective and forces us to articulate core values and priorities. This is another gift of inclusion; it allows us to share the stories and journeys of those whose paths are different than ours. It deepens our understanding and enlarges our hearts.

REAL SAFETY

To most people, being "safe" refers to freedom from danger or the threat of harm. But there are many kinds of safety. Physical safety is clearly a prerequisite for being comfortable, but psychological or emotional safety is essential for us to thrive. Part of feeling psychologically or emotionally safe means knowing that you will be accepted, that your personal characteristics or identities will not keep you from participating with others or being seen as a whole person.

Inclusion means that differences or disabilities do not automatically signal exclusion and separation. Deep safety comes from knowing that you are acceptable—no matter what.

Imagine that, as a parent, you find out that your eight-year-old has been diagnosed with juvenile diabetes. Although your first reaction would probably be one of dismay and worry, it would also no doubt signal the beginning of a sharp learning curve: how to handle medication, mealtimes, your child's feelings and self-esteem, gathering support for yourself as a parent. There would be lots to learn, no doubt. It is improbable, however, that you would say to your child, "Gee, it's been great having you in the family. But now that you have diabetes, we will be finding you somewhere else to live—a place that is especially for people with diabetes."

A similar teachable moment—for me—about inclusion occurred with my older daughter. Dalia experienced a sudden, unexplainable hearing loss when she was about two and a half years old, which necessitated her being fitted with hearing aids. Contrary to predictions that Dalia would resist wearing her hearing aids and would reject them strenuously, Dalia put the hearing aids in her ears, said, "Oh, that helps," and went out to play. She seemed very accepting of her new "equipment" and grateful for what she could now hear.

Ironically, she also taught *me* something about acceptance and my own less than fully evolved attitudes about difference. At the time that Dalia was fitted with hearing aids, she wore her hair in two little corkscrew pigtails, often tied with colored barrettes or adornments. My own discomfort with her new appearance prompted me to think about hairstyles Dalia could adopt that would cover up her hearing aids and make them less visible. But even as I tried to explore this idea with Dalia, I realized I was in trouble. How do you tell your child that there is something about her that others will find problematic or that she should seek to hide? As I struggled with this, Dalia asked, "Why would I want to cover up my hearing aids? I think it's good for people to know I have hearing aids so that they know that's why I sometimes don't understand things!" Point made, point taken. I stood humbled and corrected by my own daughter's wisdom and acceptance. If she was fine with who she was—and in fact, she was just who she had been before—then it was my issue, and I was the one who needed to work on my values.

And, not surprisingly, it has been those moments in which my professional life and my personal life have crossed paths when I have learned the most about what it means to live values of inclusiveness and compassion. When Leora was eleven, I was called as an expert witness in a lawsuit for a boy named Sam Nelson. Sam was exactly my daughter's age, and so I often told her stories about him. Adopted as an infant, Sam was a delightful child with a face full of freckles and a mop-top of blond hair. He lived with his parents, Kevin and Noreen, and his brother, Kyle, in a small town where he attended the local public school. Because Sam had cerebral palsy, he had regular physical and occupational therapy sessions, but he also stayed busy with school and Cub Scouts and T-ball. His parents did a masterful job of making sure that Sam's life was as close to typical as any other boy his age.

However, Sam's school district decided that his educational needs would be better met by busing him an hour away from home to a school that had a program for students with significant disabilities. Sam and his family were very distressed by this prospect. It was important to all of them that Sam remain in the community where he was known and loved and where he felt connections to a wide variety of people. Walking down the street with Sam and his brother, I watched as the barber greeted him and suggested he needed a haircut, as the man at the candy store spoke to him about his favorite candy, and as Sam commented that he knew that the people on the corner were moving because there was a moving van there last week.

I was asked to serve as an expert witness in a due process hearing to decide Sam's educational fate. I spent many hours getting to know Sam and his family, visiting the school that he attended and the one that the district wanted to send him to. It was very clear to me that the segregated classroom across the state had little to recommend it and that Sam could be well served in his own school and own community with adequate supports.

I would return from my trips out West full of stories of what a loving family Sam had and full of indignation that his life might be so radically altered. I clearly was "falling in love" with Sam and relishing our time together. His photo adorned my refrigerator along with pictures of my own children, my nieces and my nephews, and other special children in my life. Leora was curious about this child whom her mother was visiting and appreciating so much.

When I was invited to give the keynote address at a major inclusion conference, the whole family decided to come, and so it came to pass that Leora and Sam finally got to meet.

The conference was held in a large hotel, and the day before the conference, Sam and his brother and parents arrived at the hotel. While Kevin and Noreen and I chatted, Leora,

Sam, and Kyle played together in the hotel swimming pool. Sam, wearing water wings for support, had a wonderful time in the water, and he and Leora and Kyle played chasing games and enjoyed each other's company. After they had played in the water for more than an hour, Leora came to me with a serious look on her face. She said, "But Mama, Sam is just fine—he's a lot of fun." Clearly, she was trying to make sense of why someone somewhere would have decided that Sam couldn't be around more typical children in his community school. It didn't make sense to her; perhaps she was expecting to meet someone who seemed very different from her. "Yes," I responded, "Sam is great." She stood looking at me quietly, clearly processing something big. Then, her eyes welling up with tears, she asked in a small voice, "You wouldn't send *me* away if I couldn't walk, would you?"

My overwhelming response told her all she needed to know, but also taught me, again, about the importance of inclusion. If our children see that not everyone is valued and that some people are, in fact, in danger because of who they are, it is difficult to reassure them that *they* are safe, given the unpredictability of life and its adventures. The meaning of inclusion and the dangers of exclusion were never quite so clear to me. These are powerful lessons not just for those who are excluded but for all of us who witness this exclusion and wonder and worry what it means for us and for our own safety and community.

A commitment to inclusive schooling is a promise made to children and their families that, despite struggle and challenges, a child will not be excluded from his neighborhood school or community because he is different in some way.

Mary Falvey, an educator and inclusion advocate, makes the point that the best single predictor of whether or not a child with a disability is included is *not* the nature of the child's disability or even the availability of resources, but the level of commitment to including that child.[1]

And just as inclusion is not exclusively about disability, the lesson of safety is that we are accepted and supported in all of our identities. Inclusion asks: Will I be acknowledged as a child of color? Will I be welcomed in the school community as the son of two lesbian mothers? Will I be free from harassment as the only Muslim student in the school? In one school, for example, the teachers and administrators became aware that Ramadan was a challenging time for Muslim students; because they didn't eat from sunrise to sundown, asking them to go to the cafeteria to watch the other children eat seemed extremely cruel and insensitive. But separating all the Muslim students in a different space seemed unnecessarily exclusionary and stigmatizing. The school's solution was to designate a separate space for students—all students—to play games, read, and watch videos. The Muslim students went there for the entire lunch period, but other students finished their lunches quickly and came to join their classmates for fun activities. Differences were respected, and all students learned how to be supportive.

The deep peacefulness we feel because we know that our support and community will not evaporate when we are challenged is what allows us to learn and grow. Having friends and a community that love us even in our most troubled hour is what sustains us. Within inclusive schools, our children learn the importance of this unconditional acceptance and support.

EXCLUSION HURTS EVERYONE

Who among us does not have the experience of having been excluded? For some of us, this exclusion was based on some immutable characteristic: our skin color or our size or our religion. For others, exclusion was based on our socioeconomic level—we didn't have the "right" clothes or the disposable income to hang out with our classmates on weekends. Often our exclusion was based on a multitude of human diversity: our hair color, our size, the speed of our sexual development, our acne, or our physical skills on the playground.

I have yet to interact with any group of adults who did not, when asked, pour forth stories of times they had been excluded and the accompanying feelings. If I even mention this topic to the person I am sitting next to on an airplane or at dinner, I am flooded with stories and strong feelings. People talk about feeling sad, hurt, betrayed, angry, diminished, and invisible. Many people tell you that they still remember the exact details of their exclusion and that the feelings have stayed with them throughout their lives. Although, clearly, many of us learned important lessons from these experiences, few of us would choose this for ourselves or our children.

Many of us also remember *excluding* others, and these memories bring with them a different kind of pain. People talk about feeling briefly jubilant about evading an unpopular classmate—but then feeling guilty and ashamed. Others report feeling conflicted and confused; Marissa played with Charlotte on the weekends but told her never to approach her at school or let on that they were friends. Many of the feelings were the same whether discussing being excluded or doing the excluding: sadness and a sense of grief and resignation.

Inclusive schools give us opportunities to practice being

our best selves. Being surrounded by others who differ from us—whose characteristics may seem strange or off-putting or just unfamiliar—allows us to learn the lesson of reaching out across our personal borders to ask, "Do you want to play?" "Do you want to see what I made in art?" "Do you want to come to my house to play?"

In Vivian Paley's wonderful book *You Can't Say You Can't Play,* Paley, a kindergarten teacher, is pained to observe her young students excluding one another: "You can't be in our group"; "We don't want you in the play corner"; "You're not my friend." She wrestles with her own role in changing this behavior and approaches them with a proposed rule, asking them, "What if we had a *rule* that said 'you can't say you can't play'?" The children are wise and raise all the objections that we as adults would raise: "What if Martin hit me last time we played, and I don't want to play with him again?" "What if Shequoia and I already made a special plan to play Barbies, and LaDonna doesn't have the right dolls?"

Paley asks her children two big questions about the proposed rule: "Is it fair? Will it work?" Her book details her experiences in discussing exclusion with her young students and watching them wrestle with changing the classroom climate to be more inclusive. Paley also visits each of the other grade levels in her school, telling these "older" students that she is planning to make this rule with her kindergarteners and asking for their advice: "Is it fair?" "Will it work?"

Although the older students are supportive of her making the rule for the youngest children in the school, some of them report that it's almost too late for them—too late to change their habits of exclusion, the ways in which they have already hardened their hearts to the pain of those excluded. One girl comments, "The rule could work in kindergarten because rules are a big thing then. My little sister *likes* rules. But when you get older, some people really don't care. You're a little meaner." Another boy explained, "Look, if someone comes up to you and they're not especially your friend, and they say can I be your partner, you say no, I already picked someone else when really you didn't. Then you go to a friend and pick him." This is, indeed, sad commentary on the experience of schooling for many students.[2]

Though I do not agree that it is *ever* too late to take a strong stand against exclusion and to push for inclusion, it is true that changing a school climate and classroom norms is harder than establishing an inclusionary stance from the beginning. For that reason, inclusion is most successful when it is an organizing core value from the very start, so that a school communicates strongly at the outset: This is what we do here in this school. This is why we include everyone. Inclusion is nonnegotiable. We will all wrestle with *how* to do inclusion well, but we will not debate the general principle or commitment to inclusion.

COMPASSION

Compassion means "feeling with." The opposite of compassion is not meanness but rather indifference. Teaching children to be compassionate means allowing them to see through the surface appearance of those that surround them to the human beings inside. Compassion means treating others with tenderness and gentleness, with an open heart and a belief that the "other" is a lot like themselves.

At a recent presentation about friendships and social skills in inclusive classrooms, a teacher approached me at the break and asked for my advice. She reported that she was teaching a very inclusive third-grade classroom. Her students included students labeled as "typical"; some with the label of "gifted"; and several with special education labels, one of whom was a girl named Terri. Terri had Down syndrome, and the teacher reported that Terri had been making exceptional progress during the year and that everyone was thrilled with her growth. The last week, however, an incident had left the teacher feeling unprepared and uncertain how to respond. The teacher had returned a math test to Terri and was telling her young student how proud she was of her performance. She elaborated in great detail about how much Terri had improved and how delighted she was by her effort and progress. Another child, who was in the gifted program, wandered over. The teacher reported that the little boy listened intently as she praised Terri for her performance and then commented, dismissively, "Big deal. I got 100!"

The teacher was distressed by the boy's comment and asked me what she should explain to the boy about Down syndrome and its accompanying learning challenges. My reply, which startled her somewhat, was "Nothing." To me, this is not the occasion for explaining chromosomal abnormalities and learning differences. This is about being a good human being—a compassionate person—and people who are good human beings and compassionate people don't belittle others' accomplishments. The boy's behavior was inappropriate and unkind regardless of Terri's label or lack thereof. I told the teacher that she needed to talk to the boy about how we support our classmates, and that we can acknowledge others' achievements without feeling diminished or competitive. The boy's comment might also be the impetus for the teacher to look at whether the boy himself was receiving affirmation for his accomplishments and whether, somehow, a desperate competitiveness and the perception of a scarcity of success have crept into her classroom. This is the essence of caring, and inclusive classrooms provide many such teachable moments. Students are not automatically kind, but through our models and our active discussions about "being nice," inclusive classrooms can become teaching platforms for compassion.

By contrast, I visited an inclusive fourth-grade classroom recently. As I walked around and interacted with the students, one young boy said to me, "Guess what! Karen can tie her shoes now." I didn't understand the significance of his comment; it wasn't clear to me why being able to tie one's shoes was remarkable in fourth grade. Then I learned that Karen has cerebral palsy, and the boy's comments spoke volumes about his understanding of differences and his ability to understand that Karen's accomplishment was worth celebrating, even though he had been able to tie his shoes for years. The teacher had done a great job of helping him to understand that people are different and that there is no shortage of success or appreciation available in her classroom. He did not need to respond competitively to her achievement but could recognize that this was a big deal and worth noticing!

When I lived in Cleveland, two little girls were badly burned in a house fire. They spent months in a hospital undergoing painful surgeries, skin grafts, and rehabilitation. When they were finally released, their mother wanted to help them regain their pre-fire lives, and this involved re-enrolling them in the ballet class they had attended before the fire. The director of the dancing school said that the girls were welcome back—if they wore bags on their heads so they wouldn't upset the other children. The mother was devastated at this incredible request, so incompatible with the messages she was trying to communicate to them: that although they looked very different, they were still wonderful and lovable and completely acceptable.

One wonders, of course, whose discomfort was preeminent in this decision—the dance teacher's or the classmates'? I have had many experiences in which the children in inclusive settings have been far more understanding and accepting about differences than the adults. The children are curious, of course, but not inevitably rejecting or mean.

Several years ago, I was asked to deliver the keynote at the National Williams Syndrome Conference. Williams syndrome is a genetic abnormality that results in children who are typically short in stature, friendly, and outgoing, but who have significant learning disabilities. Children with Williams syndrome seem to be particularly verbally adept and eager to connect with others, but they sometimes miss standard social cues and can be challenged by complex tasks.

This conference was, for me, the first time that I had met so many families of children with the same genetic disorder. As I sat by the pool the day before the conference, I had delightful interactions with many of the children and their parents, and I was pleased to present my ideas about the importance of inclusion at my speech the next day.

After my speech, one mother approached me with an upsetting story. Her daughter (whom I will call Crystal) was eleven and a member of the Girl Scout troop in her community. Crystal's mother had placed Crystal in Girl Scouts so that she could have opportunities to interact socially with her classmates in an out-of-school setting. Crystal loved Girl Scouts, and her mother reported that the other girls were remarkably supportive and friendly.

When notices about upcoming summer Girl Scout camping opportunities were received, Crystal's mom checked with the other girls in Crystal's troop to find out which of the camping weeks they would be attending so that Crystal could be with girls she knew. She sent in Crystal's registration and began assembling the required "packing list" for camp. Three days before camp was to begin, the mother received a phone call from the scout leader. She was informed that there had been a meeting of the other parents (to which she hadn't been invited) to discuss the "Crystal problem," and the other mothers had said that they didn't want Crystal attending camp with their daughters because they wanted *their* daughters to have a "normal" camping experience and felt that this would be sacrificed or compromised if Crystal was there.

As she told me this story, Crystal's mother's eyes filled with tears. She couldn't understand how her daughter's participation would diminish the other girls' camping experience, and neither could I. In fact, there was little that Crystal couldn't do, although yes, sometimes it took her a bit longer. I couldn't understand why Crystal couldn't sit around the camp fire, sing songs, or do craft projects like the other girls. Was the lesson on lanyard making more important than the other lessons the girls would learn from Crystal's presence?

When I asked the mother what she had done, she told me that she had withdrawn Crystal from camp because she didn't want her daughter to be somewhere she wasn't welcome. The other girls were not consulted. Nor did the scout leader have the courage of her convictions to uphold Crystal's right to be a Girl Scout and to continue to be a part of the troop. In fact, many of the Girl Scout values involve learning about responsibility, caring, support, and community, the very lessons strengthened by Crystal's attendance and participation in Girl Scout camp. Who had the problem? Whose education was compromised by this decision? How sad to have lost this teachable moment about compassion.

GIVING AND GETTING HELP GRACIOUSLY

One of the greatest gifts of being in an inclusive environment is the multiple opportunities to be helpful and to receive help. Even the youngest of children likes to feel "useful" and valued for his contributions. Heterogeneous groups provide many occasions and chances for *everyone* to be of use.

In many settings, it is not uncommon for people to become cast in one of two seemingly dichotomous roles: a person who needs help or a person who can give help. In truth, each of us has areas in which she can be helpful or supportive of others and places in which she needs or would appreciate support and assistance.

The challenge, within inclusive settings, is to recognize that every person needs multiple repertoires of helping and being helped. Each of us needs to be able to ask for help appropriately: "Could you please help me?" rather than "Can't you see I'm struggling!" We also need to know how to offer to help in ways that preserve the dignity and independence of the person we are attempting to serve: "Do you want a hand with that?" rather than "Let me do that for you."

Once help has been offered, we each need to know how to *accept* help graciously and *decline* help with similar grace. Many of us, particularly those of us in the "helping" professions, are most comfortable when we are helping rather than receiving. This typecasting makes it difficult to establish truly reciprocal relationships and often leads to stigma, social distance, and resentment.

Inclusive classrooms can be wonderful places to establish norms and practices that are based on the belief that *all* people need help, that giving and getting help are *good* things, and that helping others creates an atmosphere of mutual support and respect.

Certainly, being around people with more obvious limitations helps us to teach children that there is no such thing as complete *independence*. All people function in community and are interconnected. Since not everyone is good at the same things, it makes sense for all people to learn to help one another in respectful ways. Being with people whose limitations or challenges are more obvious can provide an excellent base for exploring the ways in which we *all* need help and support, although probably for different things. I am a very capable public speaker, and, in that capacity, I can help others who struggle with talking in public. I am, however, a less than fully confident expressway driver, and I have learned to ask for the help and support I need: map reading, moral support, and a lookout for major intersections and exit ramps.

Inclusive classrooms also help to disrupt beliefs about who is capable and who is not and who can be helpful. A child whom others see as limited because of his physical challenges may, in fact, be a wonderful listener, have a great sense of humor, or elicit tremendous tenderness in others. Challenging hierarchies of skill and usefulness is an important gift from the inclusive classroom; there is no one so competent that she wouldn't benefit from support and help, nor is there anyone so limited that she can't be a positive force in the world through her gifts or presence.

Pushing past personal beliefs about "needing help" is critical to establishing a broader community in which we feel safe enough to ask for the help we need and confident enough about our own skills and our own roles to offer ourselves to others freely. Although I see myself as a strong and powerful woman, arthritis in my neck is teaching me that it is sometimes wise to ask others to carry things for me. I have to get beyond my own fear that I will be seen as "weak" or "disabled" if I ask for help. I must truly believe that I am giving a gift to others by allowing them to help me, and that I am establishing positive relationships with a wider range of people in my life through my willingness to name my own challenges and needs for support.

RESPONSIBILITY TO ONE ANOTHER

Closely linked to our abilities to help one another is the understanding that we are, in fact, responsible to one another. To be a community means that we do not function independently, but, rather, willingly put ourselves in relationship with others.

Many of us have had the experience of some kind of a "natural" disaster—a flood, hurricane, tornado—in which we were amazed and stunningly delighted by the ways in which others reached out to us and we to others. The recent experience of Hurricane Katrina provided numerous examples of both benevolent and generous giving and of selfish and damaging individualism. In many cases, people opened their homes to others, took in families, and provided food, clothes, and emotional support to total strangers. By contrast, in some situations, people hoarded food and guarded what they had to keep others from it, resulting in loss of life and property that surpassed the effects of the natural disaster.

Unfortunately, once the disaster is over, the storm abates, the waters recede, or the fire is extinguished, people often return to their more typical patterns of isolation and disconnection. Are there ways to teach people the necessity and joys of interconnection and mutual responsibility in the absence of a natural disaster?

Inclusive classrooms provide opportunities for recognizing that all people are connected and that a blow to one is a blow to all. In one school, when the students found out that the planned field trip to a museum involved taking a bus that wasn't accessible and that Jesse would have to stay home, they protested vehemently that either they figure out a way for them all to go, or none of them should go.

Inclusion teaches us to think about "we" rather than "I." Not "Will there be anything for me to eat?" but "How can we make sure there's a snack for everyone?" Not "Will I have friends?" but "How can I be aware of the children here who don't have friends?" When we are surrounded by people who are different from us, we are forced to ask questions that go beyond the individual and address the community and its diversity. When we have friends who use wheelchairs, we notice that there are steep stairs and no ramps. When we have friends who wear hearing aids, we listen differently to comments like, "What are you, deaf or something?" When we have friends from different religious backgrounds, we are more aware that the decorations in the mall are about only one religion, the songs on the radio affirming only one way of being in the world.

HONESTY ABOUT HARD TOPICS

In the same way that inclusion teaches students to be aware of and well educated about individual differences, it also provides a place to learn about challenging topics. We learn to talk about the uncomfortable, the unspeakable, and the painful. When I first began teaching, I taught in a private elementary school, and one of the students in the kindergarten had cancer. Rather than hiding this fact (and this child) from his classmates, the teachers used Ryan's situation and illness as an opportunity to not only educate other students, but also to help them become loving and caring allies. On the days when Ryan's chemotherapy made him tired and weak, other students took turns sitting in the beanbag chair with him looking at books. When Ryan was forced to miss school, students took turns calling him and sending home notes and drawings. And when Ryan died, almost all the children in his class attended the funeral, offering their memories and their sympathy to his family and friends.

Although very few parents would say, "I hope that a student in my daughter's class dies so that she can develop caring and support skills," the reality is that people do get sick, people do die, and people do struggle with a myriad of life situations. Helping children develop coping skills by supporting them through these difficult situations allows us all to grow as caring and compassionate people.

The desire to "shelter" our children from some of life's harsher realities must be balanced with the tremendous gifts we give them by allowing them to be comfortable, understanding, and supportive when faced with people and situations that are challenging. In one school, a young boy who required tube feeding provided the occasion for all the students to learn about the digestive system and about ways to help people while preserving their dignity and agency. In another school, a child whose religion kept him from celebrating birthdays and holidays allowed students to learn about how to keep Jarrad feeling like a valued and supported member of the classroom, even though his life experiences differed significantly.

So often, as adults, we simply don't know what to do when we are confronted by people and situations that frighten, surprise, or simply confound us. Children's willingness and eagerness to engage with the world and to find answers to their questions allows them to learn a vast repertoire of skills and attitudes that will help ensure a smooth entry into the complexities of adulthood. This is one of the gifts of inclusive classrooms.

Children learn many messages from how we, as adults, respond to differences. What we say matters, but what we *do* matters even more. As Albert Einstein said, "Setting an example is not the main means of influencing another—it is the only means." I have known quite a few teachers who have struggled with cancer, but two of them stand out because their stories could not be more different.

One teacher I knew had breast cancer and underwent chemotherapy, which caused her to lose her hair. This teacher, whom I will call Caroline, talked to her class about what was happening to her, and they became an active part of her support system, sending cards, calling her, visiting her, and then welcoming her back to school when she returned. Because of her hair loss, she had a collection of wigs that she kept at school, and each day the students would help her decide which wig to wear, often laughing and joking with her about her "new look."

Another teacher I knew also had breast cancer and lost her hair during chemotherapy. Unlike the teacher in the first story, this teacher was forbidden by her administrators to tell her students where she had been or why she had been out of school. The principal argued that cancer was too frightening for her fourth graders and that it might make them worry about their own parents. When this teacher, whom I will call Lori, found her wig itchy and uncomfortable and wanted to come to school with her bald head covered with a kerchief, she was told that this was absolutely not an option. She was very distressed that she was not able honestly to answer her students' questions about what was happening and to share her struggles and her triumphs.

Think about what the children in each class learned, not only about cancer or chemotherapy, but about love and support. The students in Caroline's class got to see a teacher who was wrestling with something big, and was doing so with courage and commitment. When she felt less than peppy, they offered hugs and support. They felt important to be part of her "team" (as she called it), and they understood the role they could play in helping her heal and repair her life. And since it is likely that many of their lives will be touched at some time by cancer, they will already have a "head start," because they won't be afraid to talk about it, share their feelings, and develop support networks as needed.

What did Lori's students learn? They learned that people disappear from their lives without explanation and return with a similar silence. They learn that even though they suspect something is wrong, no one will tell them the truth, leaving them to worry and wonder, perhaps creating even more fearful stories in their own minds. They have experienced ruptures in their lives, holes in their relationships, and an atmosphere of unexplained tension and silence. When someone with cancer comes into their lives in the future, they will have only tidbits of misinformation, rumor, or gossip, and perhaps a large residue of fear and confusion from their previous experience.

COURAGE

Although many people associate the word "courage" with dramatic acts—rushing into a burning building to save someone, for example—there are many forms of courage. And many of these courageous acts are available to us daily. We need not wait for a national emergency to act courageously or to teach our children to be courageous. Inclusive classrooms present us with a fertile field for planting these seeds of courage because they provide us with examples and opportunities for many kinds of bravery.

There is the courage to keep trying when things are hard, and the courage to move past old ways of thinking and behaving to embrace change. There is the courage to forgive those who have hurt you, and the courage to take risks in relationships, even when you face possible rejection. And, perhaps most important, there is the courage to stand up for those who are marginalized or oppressed, the courage to stand up for what is right, even when it's hard or you're the only one.

Songwriter Bob Blue talks about this particularly important form of courage in one of his songs:

COURAGE

A small thing once happened at school
That brought up a question for me,

And somehow it brought me to see
The price that I pay to be cool.

Diane is a girl that I know.
She's strange, like she doesn't belong.
I don't mean to say that that's wrong.
We don't like to be with her, though.

And so, when we all made a plan
To have a big party at Sue's,
Most kids at our school got the news,
But no one invited Diane.

The thing about Taft Junior High
Is, secrets don't last very long.
I acted like nothing was wrong
When I saw Diane start to cry.

I know you may think that I'm cruel.
It doesn't make me very proud.
I just went along with the crowd.
It's sad, but you have to in school.

You can't pick the friends you prefer.
You fit in as well as you can.
I couldn't be friends with Diane,
'Cause then they would treat me like her.

In one class at Taft Junior High,
We study what people have done
With gas chamber, bomber, and gun
In Auschwitz, Japan, and My Lai.

I don't understand all I learn.
Sometimes I just sit there and cry.
The whole world stood idly by
To watch as the innocent burn.

Like robots obeying some rule.
Atrocities done by the mob.
All innocent, doing their job.
And what was it for? Was it cool?

The world was aware of this Hell,
But how many cried out in shame?
What heroes, and who was to blame?
A story that no one dared tell.

I promise to do what I can
To not let it happen again.
To care for all women and men.
I'll start by inviting Diane.[3]

Over the last fifteen years, I have had the opportunity to sing this song for thousands of teachers, parents, administrators, and students, and the response is always personal and sometimes intense. Many people relate to this song, either because they were Diane, are the parent of Diane, have taught Diane, or remember Diane from their own school days.

At a recent early childhood conference, I sang this song for a large audience. After my presentation, a woman approached me and said, "I just want you to know—I was Diane." And she burst into tears. The woman, now in her forties, described how she had grown up rural and poor and had gone to school in clothes that did not meet her classmates' standards. Her teacher, in an attempt to create community, had sat the children in a circle. But no one wanted to sit next to this raggedy country girl, and so the teacher had placed her in the center. This woman's pain, more than thirty years later, was still real and tangible. The hurts of rejection—of being left out, teased, or humiliated—are familiar to many people.

But there is another pain as well, and that is the pain experienced by those of us who saw Diane, who saw another child rejected and teased and who didn't know what to do. This is the same pain we experience when we see a homeless person in the street or witness a travesty of justice or fair play—the sense that something is wrong here, that something should be done, and, often, that we don't know what that something is. When we see another person rejected, isolated, or turned away, we can recognize that a blow to any member of the community is, in a way, a blow to the entire community. If we are a solid unit, a cohesive group, then we cannot tolerate mistreatment of any individual.

The song also allows us to see that it is within schools that most children first experience grouping, labeling, and the valuing and devaluing of individuals. It is in school that we learn who is of worth and value and who is beneath contempt. It is in school that we learn how to befriend and how to turn away. And those lessons, once learned, have tremendous implications for all aspects of our lives. But there is also good news: it is within schools that we can teach children to act in solidarity, can teach children to have the courage to step away from the crowd if that crowd is hurting someone, can allow children opportunities to take risks and to act courageously. It is within school that we can teach children to have the courage to make a difference.

After I sang this song at a conference for parents of students with disabilities, a mother approached me and offered her story. She had received a call from the parent of one of her daughter Marissa's classmates. The other mother had asked, "Did Marissa tell you what happened on the bus today?" Marissa's mother said that she hadn't heard anything. The other mother said that the children on the bus had been harassing her son because of his size and appearance, calling him names and teasing him. Marissa got out of her seat and went back and sat next to the boy, turned to the other students, and said, "Stop that. It's not nice."

This is courage. Marissa was seven years old. What would the world be like if more of us had this kind of courage?

A picture book by Peggy Moss, *Say Something,* tells a similar story. A young girl talks about the children in her school who are teased and bullied in the classrooms and the hallways. She says, after each description, "But I don't do that," "I don't say those things." Her tone is self-congratulatory—she is not one of the "bad" students who is mean or tormenting others. Then, one day, her friends are gone, and she sits in the cafeteria alone, only to become the brunt of the jokes of a group of students. She feels terrible, cries, and wishes she could disappear. When her tormentors leave, she is surprised to see her classmates sitting nearby—friends of hers—and they have been silent. When she tells her brother what happened, she is upset at her classmates' behavior. Her brother says, "Why? They didn't say anything." "Exactly," she replies. The next day, she takes it upon herself to sit with the girl on the bus that others have excluded.

A program called the Safe School Ambassadors teaches students to become active allies to their classmates when they witness teasing, bullying, or harassment. They learn specific strategies for intervening when they can and seeking help and support when the situation is beyond their ability or safety to handle. The Gay, Lesbian, and Straight Education Network (GLSEN) also teaches students how to intervene when they see someone being teased or bullied.[4]

These programs teach students to be courageous, to take a stand against injustice and ill treatment, and to make a difference. To state that courage should be one of the defining values of our educational system and an important lesson to be learned in inclusive schools is to push hard against a system that is more comfortable talking about accountability, effectiveness, and quality management systems. But if we are going to change our schools so that they serve all children within respectful, nurturing communities, then courage is what it will take. Not only will students have multiple opportunities to tap into their own courage in heterogeneous classrooms, they will witness the courage of the adults around them as well.

Courage is what it takes when we leave behind something we know well and embrace (even tentatively) something unknown or frightening. Courage is what we need when we decide to do things differently. Perhaps we have always done ability grouping, but now decide to leave it behind and embrace more heterogeneous ways of grouping students. Perhaps we have always segregated students with significant behavioral and learning challenges, and now we decide to work toward more inclusive, integrated models of education. These changes require preparation, training, and support, but they also require courage. Courage is recognizing that things familiar are not necessarily right or inevitable. We mustn't mistake what is comfortable with what is good. When we work to build inclusive classrooms, our students will see our courage, our willingness to take risks, our need for support as we struggle with new and difficult situations.

An Australian teacher, Rosemary Williams, describes what she does as "bungee teaching." She explains, "First you take the training, then you check the ropes, then you assemble your support team on the ground—but at some point, you have to jump." You can't wait to feel fully ready or prepared, because you never will. We might identify our commitment to changing the ways schools respond to diverse learners as "bungee inclusion." We must, of course, make a plan, prepare ourselves, and gather information and resources. But at some point, we must decide that we will go ahead and do it, even though we don't feel ready, even though we are scared and insecure and are being asked to do something we have never done before.

FAITH AND HOPE

One definition of faith is the belief in that which we cannot see. Faith can also mean "trust" or "confidence." In terms of inclusion, faith can mean that even though we do not always see evidence of love, acceptance, or support around us, we believe that they are possible. We believe that the world can be different, and we believe that we can be part of that transformation. We are confident that we can make a difference, and we trust the process even though the results of our efforts may not be immediately visible.

One of the principles of the Jewish religion is that of tikkun olam,[5] literally, the repair of the world. Judaism teaches that it is the responsibility of each of us to leave the world better than we found it, to live our lives so that we have a positive influence on others. The following story, retold by John O'Brien, epitomizes the principle of tikkun olam:

How It All Began

In the beginning, before there were any beginnings or endings, there was no place that was not already God, and we call this unimaginable openness *ain-soph*. Being without end, world without end, ain-soph.

Then came the urge to give life to our world and to us. But there was no place that was not already God. So ain-soph breathed in, to make room, like a father steps back so his child will walk to him. And we call this withdrawing *tsim-sum*. Into the emptiness, God set vessels, and began to fill them with divine light, like mother places bowls into which to pour her delicious soup. And we call these bowls, *ke-leem*. As the light poured forth, a perfect world was being created. Think of it! A world without greed, and cruelty, and violence.

But then, something happened. The ke-leem shattered! No one knows why. Perhaps the bowls were too frail, perhaps the light too intense. Perhaps God was learning. After all, no one makes perfect the first time. And with the shattering of the bowls, the divine sparks flew everywhere: some rushing back to ain-soph; some falling, falling, trapped in the broken shards, to become our world and us. Though this is hard to believe, the perfect world is all around us, but broken into jagged pieces. It's like a puzzle thrown to the floor, the picture lost, each piece without meaning until someone puts them back together again.

We are that someone. There is no one else. We are

the ones that can find some of the broken pieces, remember how they fit together, and rejoin them. And we call this repair of the world, tikkun olam. In every moment, in every act we have the possibility of healing our world and us. We are each holy sparks, but dulled by separation. And when we meet and talk and eat and make love; when we work and play and disagree—with holiness in our eyes, seeing ain-soph everywhere—then, a little at a time and over a long time, our brokenness will end. And our bowls will be strong enough to hold the light, and our light will be gentle enough to fill the bowls. As we repair the world together, we will learn again and again that there is no place that is not God.

Like all things that matter, inclusion isn't easy, and, in fact, it is sometimes downright discouraging. We think we have made progress with a child or with a situation only to find that the next day brings new challenges. A commitment to inclusion requires us to keep going, to keep trying, even in the face of disappointment and setbacks.

At a recent concert, folk legend Pete Seeger explained the necessity of changing the words to an old and famous song. The song is "Somewhere over the Rainbow," by E. Y. "Yip" Harburg. At the end of the song, Dorothy sings plaintively, "If happy little bluebirds fly beyond the rainbow, why oh why can't I?" Pete explained that the reason Dorothy couldn't fly over the rainbow was that she asked only for herself. "If we only ask for ourselves," he said, "we will never get over the rainbow. It has to be all of us, and we have to help each other to get there." He proposed new words, and these have become very important to me:

If happy little bluebirds fly
Beyond the rainbow,
Why not you and I?

The implications of this reconfiguration are critical. The new words say that we are all responsible for one another. Unless we fix the schools for all our children, and the society for all of us, then we are doomed to increasing divisions between the have's and the have-not's, to building more and more gated communities and hiring more security guards who will keep those who lack away from those who have.

One of the titles considered for this book was "Just Us"—an attempt to break down the divisions we make between "us" and "them," and to say that there really is only an *us*. When we find our language sprinkled and punctuated with the language of "us" and "them," then we evidence how little we actually know about one another. We emphasize differences rather than seeking commonalities.

There is a principle in architecture called "universal design" which speaks to the ways in which buildings and other things can be designed so that *everyone* can use them. A building with a beautiful ramp allows everyone access—those who walk, those who use wheelchairs, those pushing strollers, and those with other mobility problems. The ramp doesn't have to call out, "We put this here for the disabled people"; it can simply be part of the design. We don't have to have two entrances, one for "normal" people and one for "the disabled," as though there were really two kinds of humans in the world, neatly distinguishable by these labels.

The truth is, that if we live long enough, most of us will become disabled. We will use walkers, canes, wheelchairs, hearing aids, and other devices in order to live our lives to the fullest. This is why the disability community often refers to most people as TABs—temporarily able-bodied.

Rather than hearing this as a grim pronouncement, causing us to shake and tremble, we can accept the reality that our lives will change. More important, however, we need to recognize that it is the exposure we and our children have *now* to people with disabilities that will significantly affect both how we will feel about the aging process and how others will treat us. If I see people with disabilities being treated badly, then I am terrified about becoming one of "them." If I know that folks with disabilities are still wonderful people with lots of social connections, I can accept what is happening to my own body. If others learn now how to support people who are different—with kindness, sensitivity, and dignity—then we will all be the beneficiaries of that learning in the future.

We can take the principle of universal design and extend it far beyond architecture to the concept of the "most common denominator." How can we organize the world, how can we make decisions, and how can we structure our lives so that the most people can participate? Having a ramp allows all people access regardless of their mobility challenges. Serving vegetarian food allows more people to be comfortable with the menu. Clear signage and directions allow more people to find their way.

These are the ten lessons we can learn from inclusive classrooms. We learn that fear keeps us apart but that love brings us together. It has been said that there are only two motivations in the world: fear and love. Which do we choose?

Even very young children have a propensity for social interaction and social connection. Tiny toddlers have been observed patting a baby who is crying or rushing to help another little one who is upset. Connection is our natural state, although many of our policies, practices, and institutions have built separations and walls between us. By living and learning in inclusive settings, we are allowing the natural desire for community to thrive, we are undoing our chronic sense of separation and isolation. We are giving ourselves the chance to be generous and giving. We are allowing ourselves the joy of helping and being helped. We are allowing ourselves to be as fully human as possible; this is the gift of inclusion.

Two: Challenges

Understanding and Answering Critics of Inclusion

3. "What's Wrong with What We're Doing Now?"

Having a vision is essential, and having a *wonderful* vision makes us hopeful. Turning that vision into reality is much harder and demands that we be able to respond to challenges and objections.

In fact, there have been many critiques of the idea and the implementation of inclusive education. Perhaps you have heard these, or voiced them yourself. These counterarguments come from many directions and constituencies, including from those with little knowledge about public education and from those actively involved in the educational system. It can be helpful to wrestle with the many challenges to inclusion because it helps us to articulate our own beliefs; we hear ourselves saying things we didn't think we knew, or we answer someone else's critique and realize we have addressed our own doubts.

Some of the objections to inclusive education come from deep disagreements about the purposes of schooling or from strongly held beliefs about what schools should look like and how they should be run. Inclusive education, implemented seriously, is not simply tinkering; it involves fundamental restructuring of much of schooling as we know it. It is inevitable that such radical reform will bring to the surface our divergent values and understandings, not just about schooling but about other people and the world.

Many more challenges have been practical; the task seems so huge and overwhelming that implementation seems impossible. Sometimes, because something seems impossible, we decide that it wasn't really desirable in the first place. We reassure ourselves, and convince others, that we needn't feel badly about not achieving something because it wasn't a desirable goal in the first place.

But what if inclusion is not only desirable but achievable? We would have to look carefully at all the objections to understand where they come from and how they might be addressed. Perhaps by understanding resistance and rejection, we can better promote understanding and support.

It is also possible that critics and naysayers will raise practical and logistical objections to avoid confronting more basic ideological and philosophical disagreement with the vision of inclusion. We must understand the challenges if we are to construct workable models and engage in fruitful discussion. We can also look at places and situations where inclusion is working well and, instead of dismissing these as anomalies, see them as possibilities.

It would be folly to support inclusion as something easy to do. Unfortunately, some people have attempted to "sell" inclusion to reluctant teachers and administrators by arguing that very little needs to change. Sometimes these outside "experts" and advocates have told school personnel, "Don't worry. You won't have to change a thing. You can just keep doing what you usually do, and a teaching assistant will take care of everything."[6] This is not only disingenuous advice; it also does not honor the hard work and changes that will be necessary to make inclusion successful. One would hardly try to persuade couples to become parents by telling them, "Don't worry, your lives won't have to change at all!" Rather, one would attempt to prepare them for the changes they might anticipate, connect them with other new parents and outsiders for support and advice, and remind them of the joys of parenting they anticipated in making the decision to have a child.

We rarely do things because they are easy. We commit to things and do those things because we think they are important. It would be rare for someone who has developed a successful interpersonal relationship and maintained it over time to say that it's always been easy. Rather, if he were completely honest, the narrative would be one of challenges, triumphs, and ups and downs. What would be constant would be the commitment to making it work, to navigating the challenges with love and as much grace as can be summoned.

Rather than minimizing the objections and challenges to inclusion that are voiced by both insiders and outsiders, it seems more useful to name these concerns explicitly and to consider possible responses. My hope is to respond to these challenges not with platitudes and glib reassurances, but with a different way of framing issues or concerns, one that takes into account a deep commitment to making inclusion work. It is also important to discriminate the vision and goals of successful inclusion from faulty, half-hearted, ill-conceived, or inadequately supported efforts at implementation. Though we certainly need models of inclusion that are "possible," we cannot judge a concept by its worst executions!

Even those of us who are the most committed to inclusive education (or, similarly, to democracy), we who are convinced of its moral, ethical, and educational rightness, must acknowledge that neither inclusion nor democracy is simple or easy. I think we would fare much better if what we communicated was the following: "Inclusion (or living in a democratic society) can be really challenging ... but it's worth it" or "Inclusion is sometimes really hard, but you'll have plenty of support and you won't get abandoned with your challenges." Telling teachers that inclusion won't take any more work than they are already doing, or that it won't require changes in their classrooms, or that they won't have moments of frustration and distress sets up false, unreasonable expectations. Promoting an overly simplistic, positive picture also makes those who do experience difficulties feel as though they have failed personally or are inadequate to the task.

There is an old story told about the difference between heaven and hell. In hell, all of the people have elbows that don't bend and long spoons. They try desperately to get their food to their mouths, but because of the length of their spoons and their unbending elbows, they cannot reach. They are all starving, crying with the frustration of being so close to nourishment and so unable to get it.

In heaven, it is said, the conditions are the same: long spoons and unbending elbows. But in heaven, we are told, the people have learned to feed one another. All are nourished as they interact to take responsibility for one another.

Inclusion is a bit like that. We cannot wave a magic wand and make unbending elbows bend or requisition only short spoons. We can, however, learn new ways of interacting, new ways of supporting one another, so that all can be nourished within a community of care and mutual responsibility.

"BUT I THOUGHT SPECIAL EDUCATION WAS A GOOD IDEA"

Any number of challenges to inclusion come from those who believe that we are tinkering with or significantly overhauling a system of education that is, by and large, successful. "Regular" students go to regular education, and "special education" students go to special education. But the truth is, the system isn't working for many students, and this isn't the way it's always been.

The fact that many people believe that the system is working and successful is actually a powerful indication of the problem: we have become so separated from one another that we judge situations by our own experience and don't have access to a bigger picture. Arguing that the educational system is working for everyone is a bit like a person who has a good job, a nice home, a reliable pension program and a comprehensive health care policy saying that he doesn't see any problems with the economy or any reason to change it. If we were more connected as a community, if we knew one another's stories, if we broadened our vision to look at "the big picture," then we would see that the current system isn't working for large numbers of students and that a segregated system has negative effects even for the students for whom it appears to be working.

"IT'S ALWAYS BEEN THIS WAY: WE'VE ALWAYS HAD SPECIAL EDUCATION CLASSES"

The history of special education classes—as segregated places for people with disabilities—is complex. Historically, people with significant disabilities were often completely excluded from school and education. In 1919, a child with cerebral palsy who had the academic and physical ability to be in school was denied access to public education by the Supreme Court of Wisconsin. The court ruled that the child could be denied public education because he "produces a depressing and nauseating effect upon the teachers and school children."[7] Most students with significant disabilities were simply considered "uneducable" and were excluded from schooling entirely and sometimes were placed in residential institutions.[8] To that extent, having students with disabilities in public education is clearly a demonstration of progress.

But it is also true that before the existence (and resurgence) of elaborate tracking and testing protocols, many students with milder disabilities were full-time members of general education classes—long before the language of "full inclusion." The history of one-room schools, for example, is full of examples of classes that were mixed by both age and ability. In 1919, there were 190,000 one-room schools in the United States.[9] Older, more competent students helped younger, less able ones. The teachers individualized some assignments so they would be appropriate to children at different levels, and other lessons were experienced by the whole class, with adjustments in expectations and performance for different individuals. Ironically, the educational "advancements" of separate grade levels for students, grouped homogeneously by age, has resulted in more rigid enactments of curriculum and teaching (e.g., students in third grade must be able to multiply). Though one cannot argue that each child's individual educational needs were well met in heterogeneous classrooms, there was, in spite of educational differences, an acceptance of a child's right to be in school with her age-mates. Ironically, many schools are "rediscovering" some of the same educational principles that made such schools effective, including looping (having the same teacher for more than one year) and multiage classrooms, which enable students of different grade levels to work together (and allow teachers to individualize across grade levels) while maintaining a strong community. Successful inclusive classrooms model some of these same practices, and they expect and accept that students will work on different materials and achieve at different rates.

"BUT SPECIAL EDUCATION WORKS WELL
FOR STUDENTS WITH DISABILITIES"

Although there have been many wonderful and talented special education teachers who have genuinely loved and supported their students and tried hard to educate them, it is increasingly recognized that segregating students with disabilities is highly problematic for a number of reasons.

First, students of color are vastly overrepresented in special education classes, particularly classes for the "mentally retarded." At the same time, they are underrepresented in classes for the "gifted."[10] The identification of students as deviant or deficient is, in part, a function of personal and institutional bias, unfounded assumptions about racial and ethnic groups, lack of familiarity with other cultural norms and behaviors, and a host of other issues. As such, special education has often become a dumping ground for students who are already marginalized or oppressed by the broader society. Ever since *Brown v. Board of Education* ruled that separate is not equal, it has been hard to justify the development and maintenance of classes of special education students that do not duplicate the racial makeup of the school or community. In many schools, special education has become de facto racial segregation.

Even if we could resolve the issue of overrepresentation of students of color, the research on the efficacy of special education has shown that once assigned to special education classrooms, many students do not progress enough to reenter or rejoin the "mainstream," but fall farther and farther behind, their behavior becoming more and more disparate from that of their peers and their lives more isolated from the broader community. In fact, the longer a student remains in special education, the lower the probability that he will rejoin his "typical" peers, throwing into serious question the idea that special education will help students become more fully integrated into society.

As Steve Taylor explains: "The irony is that the most restrictive placements do not prepare people for the least restrictive placements. Institutions do not prepare people for community living, segregated day programs do not prepare people for competitive work, and segregated schooling does not prepare students for integrated schooling."[11] Lloyd Dunn's early work on the efficacy of special education in 1968 called into serious question whether special education was effective for anything![12] A meta-analysis of fifty studies showed that students with disabilities who were in integrated settings did better academically and were more likely to achieve their Individualized Educational Program (IEP) goals than were their counterparts in special education classes. Students with significant disabilities educated in inclusive programs interacted more with peers, received and offered more social support, and developed longer-lasting and deeper friendships with their general education peers.[13]

Research on U.S. dropout rates shows that in the year 2000, 22 percent of students with special education labels failed to complete high school, whereas only 9 percent of students without labels did so. And although 81 percent of eighteen- to sixty-four-year-olds who had not been labeled in school had jobs, only 32 percent of those so labeled were gainfully employed.[14] This statistic has major implications for the state of our economy—implications that should worry all of us. People who are not earning wages do not contribute to the economy, and they require costly social services to survive. One of the promises of inclusive education is that more students will graduate from high school and become productive citizens. The successful inclusion of people with disabilities in future social and economic venues depends not only on the development of skills in those labeled "disabled," but in the increased capacity of those labeled "typical," to support their fellow citizens and workers. Inclusive education prepares all students to be coworkers and to offer mutual support to one another in the workplace and community.

"BUT SOME STUDENTS JUST CAN'T LEARN"

All human beings are capable of learning. We become confused if we mean that all students can learn in the same ways or that all students can learn the same things. Many of us experienced teaching in very limited ways: the teacher stood in front of the class and talked. For students who learned this way, school was usually a success experience. For students who didn't learn this way—and we are increasingly realizing how many there are—school was problematic and sometimes disastrous. People who weren't successful in school often felt bad about themselves as learners and people, and sometimes they dropped out entirely. Unfortunately, those who choose to become teachers are often (although not always) those for whom school "worked"—and so we lose a sense of how many students do not have their needs met in school.

Inclusion offers us chances to rethink the teaching/learning process, recognizing that people learn in many different ways, and that education can be structured very differently.

Although the current obsession with high-stakes tests and standardized assessment makes it even more difficult to honor and validate differences in learners, we can use the commitment to inclusion to help us rethink typical ways of teaching, narrow definitions of curriculum, and classroom practices and structures that fracture community and impede learning. We can think about ways of teaching and learning that recognize that we all have gifts and that the challenge of good teaching is to make those gifts visible, rather than to sort people into the "successful" and the "unsuccessful."

"BUT WE ALREADY HAVE INCLUSION— WE CALL IT 'MAINSTREAMING'—AND WE OFFER A CONTINUUM OF SERVICES"

It's important to understand a bit about the history of inclusion—and changing terminology—in order to understand how expectations, models, and practice have changed. The Education of All Handicapped Children Act was first passed in 1975. The law mandated that all students with disabilities, regardless of the severity of the disability, be provided with a "free and appropriate" education, and that they be educated in the "least restrictive environment" with their nondisabled peers to "the maximum extent appropriate." The law also described the need for a "continuum" of services from totally segregated placements to fully integrated ones, and required that each student be evaluated in order to determine *where* along that continuum that particular student could best be educated. The law has been amended four times, and it was renamed the Individuals with Disabilities Education Act in 1990.

Because of a huge range of interpretations of key phrases

(What is "least restrictive"? Who decides what's on the continuum and where a child is placed? How do we know what's appropriate, and who decides that?), there has also been tremendous variation in how the law has been implemented. We will look at these problematic interpretations in a moment.

Although never specifically used in the law, the term "mainstreaming" became common after the act's passage, referring to often partial placement of students with disabilities in regular classrooms. Students with disabilities had to be perceived as "ready" to participate in the general education curriculum, in what was determined to be an "appropriate" placement, and the "right" to be educated with nonhandicapped peers had to be earned by satisfactory academic achievement and behavior. Often limited to small periods of the day, and often centering on music, art, and physical education, many mainstreaming arrangements were made as private deals between teachers, when a willing regular education teacher could be found.

Unfortunately, the powerful legacies of segregated education made mainstreaming limited and problematic. Because there was often limited interaction between general education and special education teachers, it was hard for special education teachers to know enough about the general education classroom to evaluate its potential as a learning site effectively. Similarly, because general education teachers had limited or no knowledge about special education, they were reluctant to accept students with disabilities and often didn't perceive that their classroom (or they) were ready for this "outsider" to visit.

And because mainstreamed students came and went in irregular ways, their acceptance in the general education classroom was often minimal. Roberta Schnorr described how students perceived students who were only sometimes and unpredictably their classmates: they were perceived as "visitors" rather than as "members" of the class.[15] The mainstreaming model did not demand any changes in the general education classroom teacher's instruction or curriculum; it was incumbent on the mainstreamed student to fit in and adapt.

Unfortunately, it is left to individual schools and special education committees to decide what is "possible" or "appropriate," and this, of course, varies widely. It is possible for the same district to have two schools with inclusion policies that vary widely; students who move from one school to another can find themselves in radically different educational environments, thus testifying to the importance of examining the school's capacity and not just the child's needs. Placement decisions are often based as much on the willingness of a regular education teacher to accept the child as they are on assumptions about the student and his/her capabilities. Given the historical lack of interaction between regular and special education systems, the ability of educators to imagine that many students with disabilities could succeed in regular education is seriously limited.

Offering a "continuum" of services leads to the continuing exclusion of many students with disabilities. Because there are "choices" about where a particular student is served, there is little impetus for the system to change, and decisions about where a student "belongs" are a product of limited and often prejudicial understandings of what students are capable of in the mainstream. Similarly, organizing schools so that they have an "inclusive classroom" while the rest of the classrooms remain segregated and untouched is problematic. It is not uncommon for a child to be included in second grade and then returned to segregated special education services in third grade because there's no "inclusion classroom" available at the third grade. Embracing inclusion as a core value means committing to serving all students in that model, over time and consistently. It makes little sense, therefore, to talk about "partial inclusion," since this violates the basic principle of inclusion.

In his now landmark article, "Caught in the Continuum," Steve Taylor points out the pitfalls of conceptualizing the principle of the "least restrictive environment" as a continuum of services. To begin with, he asserts that "a principle that contains a presumption in favor of the least restrictive environment implies that there are circumstances under which the most restrictive environment would be appropriate. In other words, to conceptualize services in terms of restrictiveness is to legitimate more restrictive settings." In fact, as long as there are many kinds of placements, schools will look to fill each of these options with the "appropriate students," rather than look to expand the services provided to all students in an inclusive setting.

As explained earlier, more restrictive placements do not prepare people for less restrictive placements. Students are unlikely to be able to work themselves down the continuum. Being in a segregated classroom almost always makes the transition to general classes less likely and more problematic. Though certain isolated skills can certainly be taught "away" from the setting in which they will ultimately be displayed, the nature of that isolation often makes it difficult to transfer those skills or to even envision what "typical" behavior looks like. We become so focused on teaching Kevin to sit at his seat and attend to the task in front of him in a segregated setting that we lose sight of what typical fifth graders are required to do in the regular classroom. Learning to swim in the bathtub doesn't ensure that you will be able to swim in the ocean. Particularly because many students with disabilities have trouble transferring skills, it is far more effective and efficient to teach the necessary skills in settings that are authentic and normative.

Another strong inclusion advocate, Doug Biklen,[16] points out that clinical judgments about where a child should be served are almost always framed with such words as "appropriate," "necessary," "feasible," and "possible"—rather than "desired" or "wanted." We tend to make our judgments based on our (often limited) understanding of how things are generally done—and not on how they might be done if we were fully committed. The phrase "full inclusion" might more appropriately be renamed "full commitment," since this is probably the best indicator of our success in the inclusion process.

Although some inclusion programs have received major publicity and attention, we should not be misled into thinking that such policies are widespread or commonly accepted. At this time, 54 percent of students with disabilities spend most of their school day outside the regular classroom environment.

In an article titled " 'Our School Doesn't Offer Inclusion' and Other Legal Blunders,"[17] Paula Kluth, Richard Villa, and Jacqueline Thousand point out that in the more than twenty-five years since the Education of All Handicapped Children Act was passed, relatively little has changed with regard to the placement of students in more inclusive environments. In an article reviewing the history of inclusion, it was reported that by 1990, only 1.2 percent more students with disabilities were placed in general education classes and resource rooms than in 1977. The placement of students with disabilities in segregated classes declined by only 0.5 percent, from 25.3 percent in 1977 to 24.8 percent in 1990.[18] A report by the National Council on Disability (2000)[19] showed that every single state was out of compliance with the requirements of the IDEA. As Kluth et al. describe the current situation:

> Even today, schools sometimes place a student in a self-contained classroom as soon as they see that the student is labeled as having a disability. Some students enter self-contained classrooms as soon as they begin kindergarten and never have an opportunity to experience regular education. When families of students with disabilities move to a different district, the new school sometimes moves the students out of general education environments and into segregated classrooms.[20]

Carolyn Das, a parent/advocate for inclusive education, which her group calls Universal Education, writes angrily about the ways in which inclusion is avoided:

> The status quo supports the continued separation, segregation, and devaluation of our children with disabilities. Furthermore, in the status quo IT IS A MYTH that "inclusion is an option." Here is the truth for 2003: the only real options are varying degrees of segregation. Furthermore, while you can truly elect for the option of complete segregation (one extreme) you really don't have the ability to elect for what I will call "complete reverse segregation."
> Here is an example which uses food, always one of

my favorite subjects: REALLY an option: You are at a buffet. You prefer apple pie among the several choices available. You ask the server for the slice of apple pie and receive it. You have made a choice among options.

NOT really an option: You are at a buffet. You prefer apple pie among the several choices available. You ask the server for the slice of apple pie. He tells you why it's not a good idea for you to have the apple pie. The other customers agree that you are making a bad choice; apple pie is fattening, it's expensive. Even the buffet manager comes out to help convince you not to choose the apple pie.

At this point, you have asked for the pie; you have justified your reasons for wanting the pie; you may have even begged for the pie. It is clear that no one is giving you the pie. You realize that the only way to get the pie is to hurdle the service counter, wrestle the server to the ground, seize the pie in your teeth, and elbow your way out through the thronging mass of people who disagree with your dessert selection.

The bummer is, after you chew on that pie for a while, you realize it's a plastic pie. It's a fake pie! Oh, the pie isn't really meant to be eaten ... it's just an example of what you COULD have. It was just there to make the dessert tray look more fabulous, not really to be eaten!

And that is when you realize that if you want apple pie, you have to make it yourself.

That's what "inclusion as an option" is: a plastic pie on a dessert tray. It's not really an option, they just say it is. And the fact is, unless you are willing to learn to make it yourself, and to find people who are willing to learn along with you, you will never ever have apple pie. To get the pie, you must work your butt off and MAKE it happen. That is the truth.[21]

As Das says, the truth is that for many children, inclusion is not really available. The language of "least restrictive environment" and the "continuum of placements" has stood in the way of full implementation, overwhelming and undermining the spirit of the act and the intentions of those who passed it. Inclusion means belonging—right from the beginning—and not having to *earn* one's way into a less restrictive setting for a short period of time. Though we certainly still need to talk about a range of *services* that individual children need, inclusion doesn't link those services to a special *place*.

"WE'LL ALWAYS NEED SPECIAL EDUCATION"

There are those who maintain that we will always need something called "special education" and that the regular classroom cannot meet the needs of students with disabilities. Lieberman, for example, states:

> By definition, the regular classroom is where the academic curriculum rules. Consequently, full inclusion into regular classrooms for students with severe mental disabilities imposes both academic and school failure on them.... Some children with disabilities should not be in the regular classroom.[22]

And J. M. Kauffman, one of the major opponents of full inclusion, says:

The fact is, we need different instruction for different kids, and you can't have all types of instruction happening in the same place at the same time. Some kids learn very well through an exploratory approach, for example, but others don't learn well this way. Direct instruction is going to produce much better outcomes for them.[23]

Those who defend special education argue that good special education instruction is individualized and that this cannot happen in the regular classroom. Opponents of inclusion refer to inclusion as a "one size fits all" model; Fuchs and Fuchs say that "separate is better for some children, and ... to abolish special education placements in the name of full inclusion is to deprive many of an appropriate education."[24]

These objections speak powerfully to our beliefs that the "regular classroom" as it is now is the way that all classrooms will always be and have to be.

One of the biggest problems is that when we talk about inclusion, we tend to envision the classrooms we experienced ourselves, with a teacher who stood in front of a large group of students who were seated at desks, facing forward. The teacher "delivered" some kind of lesson, usually by talking. The students were expected to "absorb" the teaching and then demonstrate their understanding by reiterating some portion of it for the teacher.

So when we start imagining the classroom as peopled by a wide range of students who differ in myriad ways, we automatically see huge problems: students for whom the lesson moves too quickly or too slowly, students whose physical challenges don't allow them to take in information in the same way or demonstrate their mastery in typical ways, students whose behavior is disruptive and impedes other students' growth, students whose language skills (either fluency in a different language or communication challenges) keep them from accessing the lesson, and so on. If this is what we think of as "school," or as "teaching," then there is little wonder that we struggle to figure out how a student with a significant cognitive delay, or a student who needs to move around, or a student who is easily frustrated and agitated would participate. We must continue to ask ourselves why schools are the way they are and whether they *have* to be that way. Answering those questions will allow us to reconceptualize schooling and classrooms in ways that make inclusion more feasible.

We need to construct classrooms and lessons that allow multiple points of entry into the lesson, respond to theories of multiple intelligence and individual differences, and are "delivered" in ways that are interactive, participatory, and varied. Furthermore, we need classrooms organized so that students can demonstrate their learning in ways that accurately represent their skill or knowledge and that don't depend on proficiency in specific repertoires (not everyone will write a five-page book report).

We must also understand, as stated earlier, that special education services need not happen in a special education *place*. Students may still need physical therapy, speech and language therapy, and occupational therapy—but these need not happen in isolation from the rest of their peers or in a segregated setting.

Neither does inclusion mean that there will not be differentiation. When children are in heterogeneous groups, they are often split into groups to work on particular skills or subjects; within this context, differentiation and individualization is "normal." When many children are coming and going, being grouped and regrouped, working alone and together, then differentiation is typical and nonstigmatizing. This is very different, however, from permanent assignment to a segregated setting or cluster of students.

I completely agree that the "traditional" classroom in which all students are asked to do the same work at the same time in the same way won't work for students with a range of different educational needs. But I would argue that these classrooms do a disservice to *all* children. The child who reads faster and better than others is also not served well in a classroom with rigid, fixed expectations. The child whose home language is other than English may also fail in the traditional classroom. So will the child whose learning style requires lots of movement and activity. We can either continue to add auxiliary, pull-out services for those for whom the "regular class" doesn't work (pull-out programs for the "gifted," "English second-language learners," and "hyperactive children"), or we can fundamentally rethink how classrooms work for everyone. Full inclusion is an ideal with radical implications. Luckily, many brilliant educators have shown us different ways to "do schooling" that are more successful for all students, regardless of their labels. Part Three presents many more examples of what this looks like in practice.

"WHOSE IDEA WAS THIS ANYWAY?"

Those who challenge inclusion sometimes believe that inclusion is an unreasonable policy advocated by outsiders who know little about schools and how they operate, mainly outside ideologues and unrealistic parents who don't want their children labeled.

Though there certainly have been situations in which inclusion has been promoted by those without a firm set of foundational principles and without real experience in schools, inclusion did not spring fully formed from a vacuum. Rather, it represents the logical next step in a progression of research, practice, and litigation on the education of students with disabilities. The evolution of the inclusion movement can be traced through changes in language and terminology, as I showed in the discussion of the continuum of services and the IDEA above. Thirty years ago, our efforts were directed toward mainstreaming. When those efforts proved inadequate to the task of changing classrooms so that students would fit in, we focused our efforts on integration, trying to mesh the two separate systems of general and special education. Those efforts taught us that it was critical to construct a unified system with a range of services and to prioritize collaborative communication and problem solving.[25]

Articulating our task as full inclusion—changing existing classrooms and structures so that all students can be served within a unified system—is a natural, if profound, extension of this forward direction. The core impulse for improving the access to and quality of education for all children is part of a broader strand of educational policy and reform. The model of inclusion pushes this impulse further and denies the necessity of two separate systems, no matter how well coordinated they may be.

Though parents have certainly played an important role in the full inclusion movement, they have not acted alone. Teachers and administrators have shown great leadership in designing creative solutions to the problems inherent within pull-out programs and other forms of remedial education. In the best situations, parents and teachers have worked together to create programs that are both effective and realistic. Inclusion is a product of many people's thinking about how to create schools that meet individual children's needs but without extensive segregation and isolation.

When we call others' dreams "unrealistic," we say more about our own limitations (of imagination and commitment) than we do about those whom we criticize. It is not unreasonable for all parents to hope that their children will have meaningful relationships with a wide range of people, receive an appropriate education and be seen as valued and necessary parts of the school community and the broader society. Some people saw the Civil Rights movement as unrealistic and impossible, and they argued that racial segregation was desirable and even inevitable. Though those struggles continue, we are more conscious that our belief systems about what is possible shape our willingness to take risks and change.

I believe that inclusion represents a set of ideals—like those of the Civil Rights movement—that are deeply embedded in our shared values of decency and caring. I look forward to the day when the principles of inclusion seem as natural and widely accepted as the moral visions of the Civil Rights movement are today. John Hockenberry, journalist, talk show host on National Public Radio, and former correspondent for *Dateline NBC*—and a person who uses a wheelchair—speaks of the need for a "covenant of inclusion," a shared value that makes the idea of excluding people simply ridiculous. He says that we must erase the "not my problem" mentality—the idea that "the 'normal' people pay the taxes, and the 'abnormal' people get the services" and replace it with the deep understanding that we are all in this together, that discrimination against anyone weakens our common humanity and damages the very fiber of our society.[26]

4. "This Will Be Bad for Everyone"

Another set of objections centers on the notion that inclusion will be detrimental to all constituencies, including students with disabilities, students without disabilities, regular and special education teachers, and support personnel. Although many of these objections overlap, I will discuss each separately in order to understand the ways in which these challenges are generally linked to an inadequate understanding of the full enactment of inclusion.

"IT CAN'T BE GOOD FOR SPECIAL EDUCATION STUDENTS"

Challenges in this area can be summarized by the following objections:

• Students with disabilities won't be safe in the regular school environment; they will be victims of harassment, bullying, and exclusion.

• Students with disabilities will feel bad about themselves if they compare themselves to general education students; they'll develop poor self-esteem and will feel rejected.

• Inclusive education will leave students with disabilities unprepared for the world, without the skills they need to be successful.

Let's address these concerns, one by one.

Many of us have seen students with obvious or presumed disabilities isolated, stigmatized, and marginalized. In fact, most of us have seen students without obvious disabilities isolated and excluded as well. It is not unreasonable to worry about the feelings and experiences of students with disabilities, and no responsible person would want to set students up

85

for rejection and poor treatment. The question is, however, How do we prevent this from happening? How do we create school environments in which this is significantly less likely to happen? Do we achieve this by removing the students who "don't fit," or do we work assiduously to change the overall school environment?

Consider the story discussed earlier about the young man being teased and bullied in the cafeteria. Do we make him safer by removing him from that environment or by intensifying the security around him, perhaps by having him accompanied full time by an aide or a security guard? Or do we make him—and all of us—safer by building relationships, by making sure that students understand differences, by building a cohesive community where members feel connected, willing to stand up for one another and challenge ill treatment?

The establishment of the Harvey Milk High School in New York City, a school that serves students who identify or are identified as gay, lesbian, bisexual, or transgendered raises similar issues. If students are unsafe or ill treated in regular schools, is the only solution to remove them? Though it is understandable that parents and students may reach for segregation as a solution, given horrific experiences and prejudicial behavior, it cannot be the long-term solution to discrimination and lack of acceptance. We want to create schools in which all children are welcome, in which it is safe to be different or perceived as different, without fearing for the physical or emotional safety of some. We want schools in which parents can be confident that their child will be welcomed and valued, embraced as a member of the learning community.

If we think we can solve the problems of teasing, exclusion, and bullying by removing the targets, we will embark on an endless series of removals and segregations, which is hardly a model strategy for community building and the establishment of safe learning spaces.

The inclusion literature is full of stories of students with disabilities who have developed rich and authentic relationships with "typical" students who have grown enormously in their understanding and compassion for those who are different. The research shows that students with disabilities who attend regular schools have higher self-esteem than those who are isolated and segregated.[27] Self-esteem is not a function of how we compare to others. Self-esteem is a function of how we are responded to. I do not have to be the prettiest girl in the room or the best math student to have positive self-esteem. What I need is to be surrounded by people who give me honest and kind feedback about my strengths and challenges and who support and appreciate my growth and achievements.

Removing those who are teased or harassed is a slippery slope. Students with disabilities are not the only ones who are harassed and bullied in schools. Should we remove all students who experience ill treatment—students who are overweight, those with chronic acne, those with atypical family situations, those whose clothes are not standard, and so on? Or, do we set as our goal the establishment of a school climate that supports all students, commits itself to teaching all students about respect and mutual support and is vigilant in monitoring how students treat one another?

At a recent conference titled "Teaching Respect for All," students who identified as gay, lesbian, or bisexual talked about their school experiences. One young man whose interest in art and lack of interest in sports resulted in teasing and harassment told his story. For years, he was kicked, spat upon, urinated on in the locker room, and tormented in the halls.

His artwork was ripped up, he was shoved in gym class, and he was terrified to be in the hallways alone. The school, rather than addressing the issues that made such behavior possible, decided that *he* was the problem—and that if only he didn't look or act so differently, he wouldn't be teased. He was forbidden to go to the art room, told to modify his speech and walk, and assigned to eat his lunch in a separate room by himself so as to avoid the cafeteria. The outrageousness of this response—which is not unlike efforts to segregate students with disabilities so that they won't be targets—should be obvious. I shudder to think about what lessons his classmates learned from this experience and how little they were asked to rethink their own behavior and responses to difference.

There are also those who believe that students in special education are receiving something "special" that they cannot get in more general education settings, thus requiring segregated programming. The truth is far different. Much of what we call "special education" isn't that special (that is, that different from what general good teaching looks like), and, sadly, much of it isn't education. Because of low expectations, limited accountability, and extreme segregation, many students with disabilities do not receive the intensive educational experiences they deserve.

We also suffer from the illusion that some of what students with disabilities "need"—physical and occupational therapy, speech therapy, and so on—can be delivered only in segregated settings. Recent best practices, however, show strong support for integrating special services within more normalized and integrated settings. A student who needs speech therapy, for example, can participate in high-language intensity activities with other students who support the student through their own active participation and modeling of appropriate language. Physical therapy need not be isolated limb exercises within a special room, but can be playing a kicking and throwing game with other children within the context of physical education or recess recreation.[28]

As I said earlier, the enhanced academic performance of students in integrated settings has been established by a multitude of studies. Students with mild learning disabilities made greater gains in reading and math in inclusive settings, and students with cognitive disabilities showed improved academic performance in inclusive settings. Even those with moderate to severe disabilities showed achievement that was enhanced or at least equivalent to that made in more segregated and supposedly specialized settings.

In terms of social integration, the evidence is even more powerful. Students with disabilities in inclusive settings showed greater social competence, spent more time with peers, and were less likely to be socially isolated. For students with severe disabilities, inclusion resulted in friendships and social interactions that carried over to after-school contexts.[29]

"YES, BUT WHAT ABOUT TYPICAL STUDENTS? WON'T THEY LOSE OUT?"

Even those who can see the benefits of inclusion for students with disabilities worry that typical students will be deeply uncomfortable with classmates with disabilities, or so distracted by the process of inclusion that their own educations will suffer. They see inclusion as a "favor" we are doing for students with disabilities, at the expense of typical students. It's important to respond to each of these concerns.

Though it is true that children do notice differences, it is not necessarily true that they automatically reject or fear those differences. In fact, it is often the adults in the environment who are far more disturbed by children's differences. Children often accept differences in a matter-of-fact way when they are presented as such: "Michael's legs aren't strong enough to support his body, so he uses a wheelchair to get around"; "Carla and her brother live with their Grandma"; "Jason's body can't digest sugar, so he has to limit how much he eats"; "Mohammed practices a religion that doesn't believe in eating pork products, so that's why he doesn't eat the school lunch every day."

It is not uncommon for adults to project their discomfort on children, sometimes as a way to avoid their own feelings. I have heard many adults say, "Children could never accept a child like that" (indicating a child with a significant disability or a prominent difference) when what they *really* mean is, "I have trouble accepting a child like that."

In one school, a "typical" child invited a child with significant disabilities to her birthday party. When the parent found out the nature of the girl's challenges, she uninvited her, telling her daughter, "I'm just not comfortable having someone like that in my house." Though lamentable, this lack of comfort is also understandable, given the mother's own educational inexperience with difference. It is, perhaps, one of the best arguments for inclusive education, allowing the mother to catch up with and learn from her daughter's acceptance and compassion.

Another teacher shared a powerful story with me. One of the girls in class, Darleen, had become close friends with another girl, Margie, who had a significant disability. Darleen's mother called the teacher and asked for Margie's phone number, saying that her daughter kept talking about her friend Margie, and she wanted to invite the girl over to the house.

The teacher, hoping to avoid a situation like that described in the story above, invited Darleen's mother to come visit the class and meet Margie. Darleen's mother did come to visit, and when she was introduced to Margie, she was clearly shocked; the disability hadn't been part of her daughter's description of her friend and all they did together. The mother, with tears in her eyes, said, "My daughter is clearly way ahead of me—I'm just not ready for this." The teacher invited the mother to visit the class again, hoping that through continued interaction, she could become as comfortable as her young daughter, as capable of seeing the person and not the disability.

"Difference" is interesting and makes us curious; noticing difference and rejecting difference are not synonymous. We must not mistake "typical" for "inevitable." If we adopt an attitude that says, "Rejection and meanness are natural and inevitable," we will get what we expect. Although we have all seen teasing and exclusion, many of us have been lucky enough to also see incredible compassion and caring in so-called typical children. We have seen them gently guiding a child with physical challenges, standing up for a friend who is being treated poorly, and figuring out creative ways to include a child in a game or an activity. Our challenge is to create the kinds of school structures, policies, and practices that make acceptance and inclusion more likely than teasing and exclusion.

I visited a school that included a little boy, Daniel, who used a wheelchair, didn't speak, and had limited use of his limbs. Daniel was learning to read and write using a communication device, and his smile was winsome and communicative. I entered the classroom during individual work time, and Daniel was sitting in his wheelchair. The teacher then called the children to the rug for story time. As the children gathered on the floor, Daniel was helped into a special molded plastic chair on the floor that supported his body. As the teacher began to read the picture book, I watched as another young boy moved in close to Daniel and, witnessing Daniel's head flopping forward, gently supported his classmate's forehead. Then, with no apparent self-consciousness, he leaned over and placed his cheek on Daniel's. The message was clear: "You're okay. You're a member of the class. I am comfortable sitting next to you. I know how to support you. You are my friend." This is a lesson worth noticing and celebrating.

"ALL RIGHT, SO THEY'LL BECOME BETTER PEOPLE, BUT WHAT ABOUT THEIR EDUCATION?"

Some people worry that a more inclusive model will somehow dumb down the school as a whole, limiting student achievement and diminishing the quality of our schools. For some, the very idea that there are students with significant disabilities in their child's classroom makes them worry that, somehow, other, more "typical" students aren't receiving a quality education. Is it almost as if the presence of someone with cognitive delays, for example, somehow "taints" the classroom— or lowers the class total IQ. Others associate inclusion with having no standards; they fail to understand that all students can be held accountable for learning—although perhaps for different kinds of learning or through different demonstrations of their growth. Others worry that if the classroom atmosphere is one of inclusion and cooperation—rather than fierce competition for limited success—students won't be as motivated or achieve as highly.

A belief in the value of competition as a strategy for achieving high achievement has dominated our educational system for a long time. But as Alfie Kohn and others have argued, competition damages students all along the performance spectrum. In his book, *No Contest: The Case against Competition*,[30] Kohn shows that many of our assumptions about the motivating effects of competition are not borne out in real life. Low achievers are rarely motivated by competition because they do not perceive themselves as having a chance to win. A small number of high achievers may be motivated, but they are generally motivated to "win" rather than to learn. Competition often encourages cheating, poor interpersonal behavior, and sometimes even lower achievement (if there's a prize to the first child who finishes a book, I am unlikely to undertake reading the long and challenging book that might actually stretch me). And for all students, competition damages community and students' willingness to help one another succeed.

The evidence on inclusion's academic effects on students without labels is actually remarkably reassuring. There is no evidence that academic progress slows, and, in some cases, there is evidence that it actually increases.

Research shows that for typical students in inclusive classrooms, academic performance was equal to or better than that of general education students educated in noninclusive classrooms.[31] And, contrary to the worries of many parents of typical students, the inclusion of students with severe disabilities (when there was appropriate support) did not reduce teaching time nor create many interruptions.[32]

When teachers thoughtfully implement multilevel, multimodality curriculum and pedagogy, students at all levels have the opportunity to engage meaningfully with a full range of academic topics. As will be detailed in Part Three, multilevel teaching with differentiated instruction can be an excellent way for students at all levels to not only learn at their own level but also share their learning with others, which is directly linked to higher achievement (by teaching others what we know, we tend to learn and understand it better ourselves).

Attempts to increase the quality of student achievement —when that goal is not coupled with a commitment to *all* children—has resulted in the very opposite result: more dropouts, a lower graduation rate, and increasing failure for a larger number of students. Raising the bar without improving the teaching and resources simply guarantees that fewer people make it over the bar.

Students in inclusive settings also learn problem-solving skills that are powerfully practical and complex. How can we redesign the playground equipment so that all the kids in our class can use it? How can we figure out a communication system so that Carlton can play this video game with us? How can we write a class play that has a role for someone in a wheelchair and someone who uses a computer to talk? Learning to think inclusively—developing a mind-set that asks, "How do we do this?" not "Should we do this?" leads to extensive repertoires of creativity and innovation.

It is difficult to separate the positive effects of inclusive education on typical students into categories of "academic" and "social" because all learning occurs in a social environment. And lessons learned about interaction and support vastly expand typical students' employability and future life options.

Students view their involvement and relationships with peers with disabilities positively. Many of them comment that they have totally changed their minds about what people can do and become and that they are increasingly comfortable with a broader range of people.

Students consistently report greater appreciation of and understanding of diversity, a lesson that goes beyond disability. Elementary students without disabilities felt that inclusion programs had helped them to better understand individual differences in the physical appearance, behavior, and worth of their peers.[33] I watched as one early childhood teacher conducted a lesson on prejudice and stereotypes, asking students what they could tell from looking at a picture of a particular student. Even very young children were quickly able to see that their assumptions and their stereotypes were just that—that they really couldn't know what "that child" was like without meeting him, getting to know him, playing with him, talking to him, and so on.

One of the most pleasantly surprising consequences of inclusive education has been the improved behavior of all students in the classroom. Rather than the contagion effect that people worry about (students with a classmate with autism will learn to exhibit autistic behavior), the reverse tends to be true. I have never witnessed a student with typical behavior "becoming autistic" because he had a classmate with autism. Rather, typical students become hyperconscious of their own significance as peer-teachers and role models and acutely aware that they are important members of the teaching and learning community. The typical students who step up to the plate to become supportive and caring friends to students with disabilities are often not whom one would expect to play this role. I have seen large, "tough" sixth graders behave in amazingly tender and supportive ways with students with challenges. Compassion and understanding are not the exclusive province of high-achieving students, and, often, when a student who himself has not been extremely successful in school comes to view himself as an important person to a student with a disability—as someone who matters—his behavior improves as well.

I have seen students step in to support classmates in crisis, reassuring them when they are upset, interrupting others' teasing and harassment, and demanding fair treatment for their classmate. There is no power to change the social environment as strong as that of a fellow student who says: "Don't tease her. She's my friend."

"WHAT ABOUT THE TEACHERS?
THIS CAN'T BE GOOD FOR THEM"

Introducing the prospect of moving to an inclusive model can occasion massive resistance from both general education teachers and special education teachers as well. Twenty years ago, one would often hear that the major obstacle to inclusion was the unwillingness of "regular" teachers to accept students with disabilities in their classrooms.

But a more balanced representation of the challenge shows that special education teachers have also been resistant. Having been educated in segregated settings and having received (for the most part) certification as *either* a "regular education" teacher or a "special education" teacher, it is hard to break down the barriers of whose job is whose and what will happen if those roles are blurred or combined.

Many teachers have been prepared to teach only a narrow range of students. Graduates of teacher education programs often define themselves not in terms of *what* they teach, but *whom* they teach. This separate (and not equal) teacher education has had serious effects on all teachers. For many years, special education teachers were told, "Oh, it takes such a special person to work with those children." Although those of us who received this compliment may initially have felt flattered and honored for our work, many of us came to realize that there was a double edge to this remark and thinking. First, it implied that what special education teachers had was patience (the ability to wait for things to happen) rather than skill (the ability to make things happen). But more important, it was a remark that distanced the speaker from the recipient. It implied, "It's good that you are such a special person who can work with those kids—unlike me. I could never do that." Or, perhaps worse (and usually unspoken), "I'm glad you do that work so that folks like me don't have to."

Similarly, regular education teachers were told that they didn't have the skills or ability to work with "special kids" and that their role was to recognize children who were "different" and refer them elsewhere. They were not encouraged to take on the challenge of teaching all students. If they had taken a course in special education in their general education teaching program, it was a cursory summary of kinds of disabilities with a focus on how to recognize various disabilities and where (elsewhere) those students might be served.

This indoctrination into separate teaching roles—special teachers for special kids, regular teachers for regular kids— has often left in place very simplistic ways of viewing children, their differences and similarities, and their learning needs. It has supported the development of separate systems of education that are complementary at best, but rarely collaborative or merged. Teachers go to different conferences (special or general education), they read different journals, they often receive different professional development opportunities. The levels of separation continue far past initial certification.

Special education teachers have also been concerned that

they would lose their jobs in more inclusive models, their skills and abilities now considered superfluous or unnecessary. This is not an accurate perception of what inclusion means; teachers with more specialized skills and repertoires are critical to the inclusion process. What will change, however, is the role that these teachers play within the broader educational program. Gone are the days in which a special education teacher will have twelve students with significant disabilities and will close her door, becoming the sole educator and adult working with a small group of students.

What is true, however, is that in many districts, inclusion has not been a thoughtfully implemented program with support and resources. Rather, some districts have seized on the rhetoric of inclusion—sometimes cynically—to eliminate special education services and related supports. In the worst situations, children with disabilities have been simply "dumped" into regular education classrooms with no preparation or support. Needless to say, this practice (I would hesitate to call it a model) has often been disastrous. Teachers who have felt ill prepared and ill respected in the planning process are not likely to welcome students whom they perceive as "not belonging" in their classrooms.

Very few of us seek out opportunities to feel incompetent. Rather, we seek to avoid the situations that make us feel unsuccessful. When students are simply deposited in typical classrooms and teachers are judged by the performance of those students, there is real incentive to reject those students. Why would I want to take a student into my classroom if her challenging performance would be used to judge my competency as a teacher or determine my salary increase?

Adequate preparation and support for teachers means planning for in-service, ongoing support and resources and innovative staffing models that encourage collaboration and cooperation among professionals. Fewer than one teacher in five feels that she was "well prepared" for inclusion, and the rest say that they were moderately prepared or not prepared at all. Neither general education nor special education teachers usually receive the kinds of education they will require to be good inclusion teachers, with the skills of collaboration, differentiated instruction, and the ability to work well with parents and other community members.

Inclusive models require that teachers work together. In some models, for example, a classroom of third graders might be taught by two teachers, one trained in general education and one in special education. Other adults or paraprofessionals will often be in the classroom as well, and other educational specialists (speech, occupational, and physical therapists, for example) will participate. Teaching in isolation is not possible in inclusive models. As such, teachers need to learn extensive repertoires of collaboration, co-teaching, and communication to plan and teach effectively with others.[34]

As a teacher educator who prepares teachers to work in heterogeneous, inclusive classrooms, I take the position that working with students with disabilities is *part* of the more general work of good teaching and is thus available and possible for all teachers. Segregating students with disabilities who are then attended to by "special people" does not bring us closer to the vision of inclusive communities in which a wide variety of people interact comfortably with one another across differences and boundaries.

Some teacher education programs, however, are disrupting these dichotomous ways of preparing teachers and are structuring their programs to prepare teachers for all learners. At Syracuse University, for example, where I teach, the Elementary and Special Education Inclusive Program (the only undergraduate teacher education program offered) operates from the assumption that there are not two kinds of learners, regular and special. Rather, there are huge differences in the learners who present themselves in our classroom, and we must learn to teach for diversity—anticipating it, valuing it, and addressing it in our classrooms.[35] Diversity and a range of learners must be regarded as both inevitable and desirable, not as something to lament or eliminate. The students who graduate from Syracuse's Inclusive Education Program are dually certified in "regular" and "special" education and have the skills, attitudes, and commitments required to work in and toward more inclusive educational placements.

"WON'T SCHOOL STAFF NEED TRAINING AND SUPPORT TO IMPLEMENT INCLUSION?"

The answer to this question appears contradictory. Yes and no. All school staff (teachers, aides, related services providers, administrators) need extensive training and support to make inclusion work. But these are not, for the most part, information or resources that are any different from the general education and support that is demanded by effective schooling in general. Teachers need ongoing support to develop and implement multilevel, participatory, relevant, and engaging curriculum; they need a repertoire of teaching strategies that reach a broad range of learners and actively engage students; and they need support for creating classroom communities that are welcoming and supportive of all students.

In the early days of inclusion, it was common for educators to assume (and sometimes demand) that they needed extensive training in disabilities to be successful inclusionists.

Though it is certainly true that some general understanding of differences in physical and learning abilities is important, front-loading inclusion with extensive training in particular areas of special education is less effective than an overall structure and atmosphere of support.

Imagine taking a parenting course before your child was born that covered not only labor and delivery (or the adoption process) but extended through toilet training, managing transitions to school, dealing with drugs and alcohol with your teenager, and so on. Such a training program would be overwhelming (and endless). Rather, what we need as teachers, as with parents, is some general principles and preliminary information and then *ongoing access to support*. It is difficult to teach everything beforehand because children who come into our classrooms are individuals; learning generalities about "children like this" may impede our abilities and willingness to be flexible and accommodating. Dealing with stereotypes also short-circuits any openness to grasp the uniqueness of a particular child's needs. Teachers need the equivalent of a 1-800 number they can call when they run into challenges and problems. They need active administrative support, and they need colleagues with whom to problem solve and collaborate. Teachers especially need to believe that they have not been abandoned with the challenges of inclusion. Teaching, like parenting, can be extremely lonely, and one of the biggest obstacles to successful inclusion is the feeling that "I'm all alone with this, and no one knows or cares that I'm struggling and need support." Countering this sense of isolation is perhaps the most important gift we can give teachers and administrators who are pursuing inclusive schools.

"OKAY, BUT WHAT ABOUT PARENTS—
THEY CAN'T POSSIBLY SUPPORT THIS, CAN THEY?"

We are not surprised, perhaps, that parents of students without disabilities may be concerned about inclusion for many of the reasons already articulated, but parents of students *with* disabilities do not automatically embrace inclusion, either. There are challenges for all parents.

We are all products of our experiences. Adults who grew up with minimal or negative experiences with those perceived as "different" often struggle to understand inclusion. If you are one of those people who grew up with the special education classroom buried deep away in your school—often in the basement—then it may be hard to imagine "those children" a part of a general education classroom now. We tend to reason: "Well, if they were that like me—and not so different—why did I have nothing to do with them?" Reviewing our own past histories with difference and disabilities can make us question our own memories and perceptions.

Many adults, however, realize that we live in an increasingly multicultural, diverse world, and they recognize the importance of raising children who move fluidly across cultures and are comfortable with a wide variety of differences. Their attitudes toward inclusion often shift when they can see the "bigger picture." In one school in Wisconsin, for example, the classroom that included children with hearing impairments and taught all children sign language became a much sought-after placement for typical, hearing students. One parent said that she worked with a man who was deaf and was eager for her son to know sign language because she realized the limitations in her own life. Another parent had a sibling who was deaf and wanted her daughter to be able to talk with and interact with her aunt. As soon as we break down false notions of us and them—those of us who are "normal" and those of us who are "different"—we see that diversity is all around us. Having multiple repertoires—be they second languages, the ability to problem solve, or comfort with difference—is always desirable. Inclusion is "value-added" education.

Parents of students with disabilities who have become convinced that their child can only be safe, loved, and educated in a segregated special education setting may also have difficulty adjusting to the idea that inclusive education is a better model. No parent wants to risk his child's happiness or safety or self-esteem, nor does any parent want his child to be forced into a setting in which teachers and students may be hostile. So given the choice between what is described as a hostile general education setting and an accepting special education setting, it is not surprising that some parents of children with disabilities feel that segregation is a better idea.

Marcie Roth, a longtime disability and inclusion activist, relates her painful decision to put her young son in a segregated school after trying for years to have his needs met in an inclusive setting.

Although her son, Dustin, had an IEP, it was not implemented—not for one day. He received no behavior support plan, no keyboarding, and no extra set of books for home. The testing he received was inadequate. Rather than implement Dustin's IEP, as required by law, the school system decided it "couldn't" serve him and wanted him placed in a segregated school in another county. This is where Dustin is now, at a cost of $50,000-plus per year to the taxpayers of Marcie's own community.

A *Washington Post* reporter interviewed Marcie in early 2003 about the frustrations she had encountered:

[Dustin's] last report card had shown N/G, which meant no grade, in every subject except physical education, where he received the single A that apparently qualified him for the honor roll.

Dustin was bragging about the award in his science class . . . when his teacher interrupted him. "I can't allow you to be dishonest in this class," the woman said. "You didn't make the honor roll, Dustin."

When the boy objected, the teacher apparently forgot she was dealing with a fragile ego in a room full of children and said, "You couldn't have made the honor roll because you failed my class."[36]

Marcie continues the story:

I bet you're wondering why I didn't take legal action to force implementation of the IEP. I tried. I did as much as I could. A few wonderful people stepped up to help me, but I was unable to afford the legal battle I needed to fight, and I was well aware that even with adequate resources to spend on a lawsuit ($50,000 or more), I was likely to lose anyway. There are very few legal resources for people like me. Just last year, I spent $8,000 out of pocket, paying expenses for professional experts to attend meetings—professionals I would have needed to use as expert witnesses in a hearing had I pursued a lawsuit. . . .

While I was struggling to pay experts to attend meeting after meeting, as I fought for my child's right to an education, my school system was paying lawyers $650 an hour or more to fight parents like me. Where did they get that money to spend? Taxpayer dollars, of course! They used my taxpayer dollars—yours, too—against my child.

Dustin's neighborhood school should be able to include him. But they have proven that they have neither the will nor the way to do it. I am a staunch inclusionist who now says: You're wasting your breath on that argument.

I am far more aware than most that it really is possible to get inclusion right. I'm also far more aware than most of just how wrong "inclusion" is when it's not right.

My child will no longer pay a price for my ideology. He's paying a different price right now—the price of being segregated from his nondisabled peers. I get to live with the guilt of allowing this. Supporting it, even.[37]

Marcie Roth's powerful story makes clear that issues of social justice are central to the struggle for inclusion. Parents should not be put in the position she was—having to choose between what she feels is right for her son's education and the cost of expensive litigation.

After meeting and talking to hundreds of parents of children with disabilities, however, I have yet to meet one who did not dream that her child would someday have friends and connections with the broader community, not just with the community of other children with autism, for example, or the community of other people who are blind.

A statement by the Alliance of Inclusive Education (Allie), a network of disabled people, parents of disabled children, and teachers and other professionals who support inclusive education, indicates some of the long-lasting dangers of segregation for children with disabilities:

> Most, if not all parents, start out wanting inclusion, i.e. they want their child to be welcomed into the world and given the respect and the resources they need and deserve. Unfortunately many families do not experience this. The uneven nature of the development of inclusive services from one [area] to another—indeed one school to another—means that many parents still experience hostility and rejection in their search for inclusion. Some of these parents find a better mainstream, whilst others are drawn into the segregated system. Here, they may find a sense of safety and security which was missing from previous placements. If they have been sufficiently seduced by the medical model they may feel that their child will be made "better" in the special school because of the promise of more therapies and specialist input. Our experience also is that the parents who walk down this road realize, too late, that it does not do what they thought it would. Their young adults are completely isolated from their local communities, do not have social skills, have a very poor level of education, and are channeled down a route of further segregation, discrete courses, or residential placements.[38]

In some districts, the pretense of inclusion has been used to cut costs and reduce services to children with disabilities. Some children are dumped into classrooms in the name of inclusion when, in fact, nothing is in place to make them inclu sive other than the presence of children with significant disabilities. We can hardly say, given such a scenario, that "inclusion doesn't work." We can say only that unthoughtful school restructuring, irresponsible fiscal management, and lack of support and change don't work. And that's not news.

Sometimes parents have good reason to fear that the rhetoric of inclusion could mask a real reduction in services. Inclusion without resources, without support, without teacher preparation, without commitment, without a vision statement, without restructuring, and without staff development *should* worry all of us. We know enough about what it takes to do it right, and we better do it right.

5. "Yes, but You Don't Mean . . ."

Even when people embrace inclusion as a concept and a goal, many pragmatic objections remain. Yet if we look carefully at these objections, we can see that our assessment of whether something is or is not realistic is closely related to our level of commitment.

"BUT NOT FOR *THESE* KIDS"

Although the concept of inclusion makes sense to some people for some children, the idea that we are talking about *all* children is more challenging. I am often tempted to ask, "What part of 'all' don't you understand?" Surprisingly, however, people have very divergent views about whom inclusion isn't right for. Part Three will examine more examples of how many kinds of students can be successfully included, but first we must understand the challenges.

Students with Significant Disabilities

Many people are comfortable with the idea that students with mild disabilities can be included easily, but are unable to see how students with more challenging educational needs can be part of a "typical" classroom. Because of prevailing beliefs about what students with significant disabilities need—often conceptualized as intensive therapies—it is hard to conceptualize how a regular third grade or a ninth-grade health class could be educationally appropriate.

As we will see in Part Three, however, many of the individualized educational goals for a student with significant disabilities can easily be incorporated into a typical school day. A student with communication challenges can be presented with numerous opportunities to express himself, to make choices, to indicate preferences and responses. A student with limited mobility can still participate in many classroom activities and meet her movement goals within the context of authentic learning activities.

Both research and best practice have shown that even students with severe and multiple disabilities learn more with the constant stimulation offered by the regular classroom and by the many spontaneous opportunities to interact with more typical peers. It is very difficult for a special education teacher working with students in a segregated setting to provide the stimulation and diversity of experiences found in typical classrooms. Research has shown that students labeled as having "severe disabilities" who receive their special education services in regular classrooms—surrounded by nondisabled peers—achieve higher gains in independent behavior and social competence than do those in self-contained classrooms. These findings challenge the notion that students with significant disabilities need to be in self-contained settings to achieve their IEP goals.

To make sense of having students with significant learning differences as members of an inclusion classroom, we must carefully rethink our assumptions about intelligence, ability, and aptitude. It is not uncommon to hear someone say, "What is a student with an IQ of 45 going to get out of a biology class?" We must question what it means to have an IQ of 45, and we must evaluate the testing that yielded that score. And we must also wonder: What if we're wrong about this student's capabilities? Which would be a worse mistake: to have had high expectations and exposed the student to much more than he could actually understand, or to have had falsely diminished expectations and deprived the student of learning opportunities? This concept is called "the least dangerous assumption," asking us to make assumptions that have the least potential for doing damage.

Anne Donellan explains this concept as follows: " 'Least dangerous assumption' states that in the absence of absolute evidence, it is essential to make the assumption that, if proven to be false, would be least dangerous to the individual."[39]

Recent research on persons with autism is full of examples of the incredible academic skills of people who were assumed to be "not paying attention" or who appeared so emotionally removed that teachers had no idea they were learning.[40] Biklen describes this stance—that we should assume that people are intelligent even when we are not sure—as "the presumption of competence." In an article about assumptions about intellectual ability and disability, Sue Rubin, a young woman with autism who types but does not speak and who is now attending college, writes:

> When I was in school autistic people like me were usually placed in separate schools or special day classes with other disabled students [and] were not allowed to learn academic subjects. Because of the way we move and our lack of speech we were assumed to be retarded. I was thought to be retarded [but] all this changed... once I could type without support.... My very existence challenged beliefs about mental retardation. Able to type independently... my presentations [at conferences] were acts of advocacy.... When people see me they are forced to admit that their assumptions about mental retardation were wrong.[41]

Even when a student's skills appear clearly divergent from those in the regular classroom, we shouldn't assume that biology is the only thing that can be learned in a biology class. A typical 45-minute biology class provides multiple opportunities for many kinds of learning, including social skills, communication skills, mobility skills, and so on.

Students with Mild Disabilities

Conversely, there are critics of inclusion who do believe that it makes sense to include students with significant disabilities—but not those with mild disabilities. These educators look at a student with significant disabilities and see his needs as *so* different than those of typical students that it is reasonable to assume that he is learning *something*. But these same critics believe that those with learning disabilities and other relatively mild learning challenges need very specialized instruction and will not benefit from inclusive practices. What these critics are often responding to are the ways in which students whose educational needs differ from some standard are often ignored or unattended to in typical classrooms. In classrooms in which there is little or no differentiation, it is true that students with learning disabilities will not fare well. But, again, this is not the goal—to leave typical classrooms unchanged and unenriched and simply place all students within a common space, hoping they will learn.

Differentiated instruction (as we will explore in Part Three) involves attending to multiple ways in which students can acquire knowledge, participate in learning activities and demonstrate mastery of the content. Including students with learning disabilities in typical classrooms involves paying careful attention to learning styles, to pacing, to instruction, to the conditions that support learning for various students, and to creating an atmosphere that embraces diversity and alternative paths to similar goals.

Students with Behavioral Challenges

This is the group for whom inclusion is most typically challenged. It is frightening to think of having a student in the regular classroom who is angry, violent, or displaying other inappropriate social behaviors. It is important to remember, when thinking about students like this, that critical support services would need to be provided, and that teachers should not be abandoned with any child who is challenging. Again, dumping a child on a teacher's doorstep with minimal or no support is *not* inclusion and shouldn't be mistaken for thoughtful, collaborative educational programming.

When a child with behavioral challenges is in the regular classroom, there is typically a teaching assistant in the room to support the classroom teacher and help the student to participate appropriately in the class. A collaborative team would learn more about the contexts in which the behaviors occur and would design ways to change these circumstances. Then a positive behavioral plan would be developed with a focus on teaching appropriate social skills, and not just meting out consequences for negative behavior. Keeping *all* children safe is clearly nonnegotiable, but I have also seen "typical" children learn to be amazingly understanding and supportive of a child who is angry or upset.

David Pitonyak, a gifted and compassionate educator who works with people with behavioral challenges, says that he believes that loneliness is the number one cause of difficult behaviors. "It is not the only cause, of course, it is just the most common one. We are relational beings, and the absence of meaningful relationships makes us sick."[42]

Given that analysis, the strategy of isolating students with challenging behaviors simply increases the chances that they will feel lonely, apart, and unconnected—and that this ungroundedness will exacerbate any inappropriate behaviors. Norm Kunc[43] argues strongly that according to Maslow's hierarchy of needs, unless students feel a strong sense of belonging, they cannot learn new skills. Making students earn their right to be in the mainstream of education often dooms them to eternal segregation, because they cannot learn when they do not belong.

As to ensuring students' safety, it's important to recognize that placing all the students who have behavioral challenges and inappropriate behaviors together in one classroom is likely to be counterproductive. Students placed in segregated settings often imitate the inappropriate behavior of their classmates. Students with behavioral challenges tend to perform better in classrooms with typical role models, conscientious and consistent social skills training, and an atmosphere of support and community.

Gifted Students

There are some who argue strenuously that students with accelerated skills and performances—those who are labeled as "gifted"—also need segregated programs and cannot have their educational needs met in a typical classroom.

I have argued elsewhere[44] that many of the characteristics of typical classrooms that make them inappropriate for children with disabilities—and must be changed to make inclusion work—are the same characteristics that make them inadequate educational settings for students identified as gifted. *No* student benefits from rigid, lockstep curricula with no differentiation, a classroom atmosphere that is hostile to individual differences and encourages competition and negative comparison, limited student influence on decision making and classroom processes, and restrictive forms of pedagogy.

Further, many of the same changes that make inclusive classrooms function well for students with disabilities also make them far more responsive and appropriate for students whose performance is above average. As will be discussed in Part Three, it is possible to construct curricula and pedagogical practices so that all students are engaged and have their educational needs met at their level but within a context of shared community. Being different need not lead to segregation and isolation.

Many students who are labeled gifted report that they don't like being pulled out of the regular classroom or the stigma attached to being "too smart." But some students whose performance is atypically proficient also experience negative sanctions within the regular classroom, including teasing, social isolation, and exclusion.

The solution to these concerns need not be removal for students at either end of the performance spectrum. All students have the right to feel safe and valued within their classrooms, teased neither because they read "hard" books nor because they are just learning to read "easy" books. Safety for students identified as gifted cannot be achieved by their removal. It must come from reconceptualizing and restructuring the regular classroom so that differences are normative and individual gifts and challenges are accepted as part and parcel of the classroom makeup.

"BUT WHAT ABOUT ALL THESE
OTHER SCHOOL MANDATES?"

Public schools are under tremendous pressure as I write this book. Federal, state, and local requirements demand massive changes in educational policies and practices, and many of these are directly incompatible not only with inclusive education, but also with many other reforms identified as "best practices" within education.

Those who passed the No Child Left Behind Act claimed that an intensive program of testing and sanctions for underachieving schools would increase schools' accountability to learners and improve the quality of public school education. In fact, the flaws of this movement have been extensive and are well demonstrated.

In many states, the sole gauge of student progress has been reduced to reading and math scores. Many schools already are narrowing instruction to what is tested. Some schools no longer have time to teach social studies or science and have eliminated their music, art, and physical education programs and many extracurricular activities.

NCLB requires that schools show that they are making "adequate yearly progress." If they don't, clear sanctions are imposed. But virtually no schools serving low-income children have cleared these hurdles, and many successful schools have been set up to fail. Sanctions designed to force school improvement have often done the opposite, shuffling inadequate resources, pitting parents against teachers, parents against parents from other schools, and schools against each other.

Ironically, NCLB has been particularly deadly for students with special education needs. Although some hoped that the requirement that *all* students make annual yearly progress would make schools more accountable for teaching students with disabilities, this hasn't happened for the most part. Instead, forcing students with severe cognitive disabilities and other learning challenges to take the standardized tests has limited schools' abilities to respond to students as individuals, doomed many students to failure, and, perhaps most seriously, led schools to push out students with disabilities because they lower the school's reported progress. When schools are held "accountable" for all their students' learning (with little if any flexibility or accommodation), then they are reluctant to include students who will "lower their averages" or put their school at risk of being labeled a "school in need of improvement."[45]

Many other best practices in education have also been severely challenged by the increased focus on standardized and high-stakes testing.

The recent focus on high-stakes testing has significantly curtailed the ability and willingness of many teachers to expand their curriculum. The age-old question "Will that be on the test?" now defines teacher behavior as much as it does student concern. In Massachusetts, teachers constructed a graveyard of lost educational opportunities——things they used to include in their curriculum but had to eliminate because of the current focus on standardized testing. The teacher who used to take students on extensive field trips to museums and art galleries, the teacher who created a yearly Shakespeare festival with all students, and the teacher who had her class collect water samples from a nearby pond to study water pollution and state ecological policies all expressed their dismay and distress. It was clear to them and to many parents that the new testing policies and practices directly affected the quality of their work and their relationships with students and kept them from teaching what they believed really mattered for their students.

This narrowing of the curriculum has been bad for all kids, but it particularly has challenged the ability and willingness of classroom teachers to meet a wide range of needs in the classroom. Inclusion is much easier (as we will see in Part Three) in a classroom in which the curriculum is rich, diverse, authentic, and engaging. A classroom mock election, the creation of a classroom restaurant, the production of a play—all of these allow many types of students to participate at many levels. When the curriculum is reduced to drill-and-spill worksheets, it is much harder to include a diverse range of learners. When we construct a single continuum of achievement, we produce few winners and many losers. We lose the gifts of many students whose skills aren't tested and thus aren't valued. And we often lose sight of the children themselves.

Recently, a teacher approached me in tears; there had been repeated racial incidents on her school's playground, and she felt an urgent need to engage students in discussion and action related to creating safe schools and accepting communities. But when she brought this imperative to the school administrators, she was reminded that the statewide standardized tests were coming up soon and was told that there simply wasn't time to address these issues with students. She was told that she must concentrate exclusively on academic achievement so that the school would look good on the tests and not risk funding cuts or negative publicity. Her attempts to explain the relationship between students' sense of safety and belonging and achievement scores were dismissed as interesting but not compelling. A focus on high stakes testing has also made it very difficult for many teachers to focus on issues of classroom, climate, social interactions, and social justice.

The bad news is that narrowing the curriculum, focusing exclusively on academic achievement, and measuring success exclusively on the basis of standardized tests have diminished schools' abilities to reach a broad range of students. The good news is that careful, conscientious implementation of inclusive education can address many of these same concerns. Effective inclusion could improve the schools for all students and truly make an educational system that left no child behind.

"BUT NOT HERE/NOT NOW"

Even those who embrace inclusion may argue that they're not ready or that theirs isn't the "right" school or district to begin with. The concept of readiness is problematic in many ways because it often holds us back from experiences or opportunities we might benefit from. Our fears keep us from feeling "ready," or we adhere to some misguided notion of "readiness" that says that if we were really ready, we wouldn't be nervous or worried. We don't feel that we are ready for inclusion, and we don't feel that our students are, either.

Who among us felt genuinely "ready" to become a parent, or to begin our jobs or enter our professions? Often, even when we thought we were ready, it turned out that there were challenges and complexities we didn't even know to be worried about. Though advanced preparation and training are essential, it would be a mistake to think that we could learn everything (or even predict everything we need to learn) or that we will ever feel ready.

Others will argue that the students just aren't ready for inclusion—that they will need years to be prepared for this model. The concept of "readiness" has been critiqued in the context of students' learning because it has often resulted in holding students back from experiences and teaching that they were deemed "unready" for. Sometimes this assessment of students' readiness was based on misperceptions, stereotypes, and narrow thinking about who could benefit from what teaching (for example, "There's no point in having this child go to see the Shakespeare performance because he's not ready for that").

The reality is that we can't accurately predict when anyone is ready to profit from a particular experience, especially if we broaden our understanding of what is being learned. A four-year-old at a Shakespeare performance may come away with great appreciation for the costumes or scenery or with deep fascination with stage mechanics even while she does not understand Shakespearean English. A person with physical limitations may derive great benefit from even partial and distinctive participation in an aerobics class, even though he is not able to duplicate all the moves demonstrated by the instructor. Waiting to feel ready can keep us from taking risks and stretching our sense of what's possible.

It is also easy to believe that there is some place—some school—some other community—that is better suited to embracing inclusion as a guiding value. Somewhere there must be schools with plenty of resources, few children with challenges, perfect teachers, effective administrators, and supportive parents who could more easily be persuaded to embrace an inclusive education philosophy.

The truth is that we must each start where we are. Every school, every community, every situation is unique and different, and each has its own challenges or complications. Believing that inclusion is something we can "add on" when we have everything else in place misses the point that inclusion is about everything we do and how we do it. Inclusion is not a little tinkering to the system, or a slight modification in service delivery models. Embracing inclusion means looking critically at every aspect of our classrooms and our schools— curriculum, pedagogy, climate, staff preparation, and community involvement—and a commitment to inclusion must be part of every vision we have and every change we make. In fact, once our commitment to inclusion becomes clear, it will help us to make a whole host of other decisions, weighing each against some key questions: "Will this bring our community together, or will it further fragment and separate people?" "What values will we be teaching our children through this decision, and is it one we are proud to articulate?" If we embrace inclusion as a core organizing value of our educational system, then we stop asking "When?" and start asking "How?" These different questions take us in very different directions.

Planning and preparation will certainly help us to make inclusion work well. And there is no denying that adequate lead time and thoughtful groundwork improve the quality of what happens when we move to a more inclusive model. But it is also true that no teacher, school, or district has ever felt truly ready to begin inclusion, and what is most necessary is ongoing support and commitment. Even schools that are well known for their inclusion programs acknowledge that there are always new issues and concerns to deal with. Although some aspects of the inclusion process become easier, they still require time and planning because every child and every situation is different. What we can have in place, however, is a commitment and a process that enables us to problem solve more effectively and with greater cohesiveness.

I recently spoke to teachers in a district that had made very little progress toward inclusion, even though the district's vision statement included the ideas that "all children can learn" and that "diversity must be nourished within the schools." It became clear that some leaders were hoping that if they just ignored inclusion long enough and hard enough it would go away. It is hard for me to imagine, however, that parents who fought so hard for the right to have their children included in general education classrooms will willingly (and quietly) go back to segregated programs. And teachers who have experienced successful inclusive, collaborative models are not likely to want to return to a segregated system, either. Whether our society is willing to commit the money and the people necessary to do inclusion well is another question—and it is this question that brings us to the very heart of our values and our priorities about children and their educational futures.

Norm Kunc argues that we must understand that inclusion is a moral and political issue. He writes:

> The process of integrating an exceptional student is often thwarted by a teacher's or a principal's fear of students with disabilities. Yet, the only reason why educators are afraid of students with disabilities is because they have never been exposed to students with disabilities. The only way educators will be able to overcome their fear is if students with disabilities are integrated into the regular schools, which is unlikely, as educators are afraid of students with disabilities. At some point, this vicious circle has to be broken

by educators who admit their fear of students with disabilities yet still decide to maintain a commitment to integration. . . . The only way one can overcome one's fears is to work through the fear.[46]

The best way to answer the challenges articulated in this section is to examine what schools need to be for inclusion to work. This represents the need for major restructuring and overhaul. If inclusion were simply something we could add— "we'll do inclusion on Thursdays from 2 to 3"—we would be there already. What makes inclusion powerful as an organizing strategy is exactly what makes it challenging. It requires a critical examination and reconceptualization of all aspects of school: the curriculum, the pedagogical practices, the ways in which teachers and students are supported, the ways in which learning is assessed, and the overall articulated goals of the educational process. This is a tall order!

The next chapter attempts to paint a picture of what inclusion in action looks like. By reading about real schools, real teachers, and real students, we can begin to envision the practical manifestation of our goals. We can identify further challenges and strategies for overcoming obstacles.

Interlude

Inclusion in Action
Micah's Story

We have articulated a vision and identified the challenges. Although the vision may feel compelling, the challenges are real and sometimes feel overwhelming. But, if we remember why we are doing this, and that it is possible, then many more things also feel possible.

This section allows us a glimpse at what happens when inclusion goes well and a school is able to realize possibilities for improving everyone's education through a process of thoughtful, conscientious inclusive education.

Micah Fialka-Feldman is twenty-one years old and currently a college student.[47] Many people believed that going to college would be impossible for a child like Micah, who is labeled as having a cognitive disability. His mother, Janice Fialka, an educator and poet, now spends much of her time helping other parents and educators realize the critical importance of inclusion and working as an advocate for students with disabilities and their families. As a mother, Janice has had her life turned upside down by her son's multiple diagnoses and the ways in which others saw her son. She expresses this experience through poetry, prose, and public speaking. In the poem below, she addresses those who work with children with disabilities and meet their parents through "case conferences."

Advice to Professionals
Who Must "Conference Cases"

Before the case conference,
I looked at my almost five-year-old son
and saw a golden-haired boy
who giggled at his baby sister's attempts to clap her
       hands,
who charmed adults by his spontaneous hugs and hellos,
who often became a legend in places visited
because of his exquisite ability to befriend a few special
       souls,
Who often wanted to play "peace marches"
And who, at the age of four,
went to the Detroit Public Library
requesting a book on Martin Luther King.
After the case conference,
I looked at my almost five-year-old son.
He seemed to have lost his golden hair.
I saw only words plastered on his face,
Words that drowned us in fear,
Words like:
Primary Expressive Speech and Language Disorder,
Severe Visual Motor Delay,
Sensory Integration Dysfunction,
Fine and Gross Motor Delay,
Developmental Dyspraxia and RITALIN now.
I want my son back. That's all.
I want him back now. Then I'll get on with my life.
If you could see the depth of this pain
If you feel this sadness
Then you would be moved to return

*Our almost five-year-old son
who sparkles in sunlight despite his faulty neurons.
Please give us back my son
undamaged and untouched by your labels, test results,
descriptions and categories.*

*If you can't, if you truly cannot give us back our son
Then just be with us
quietly, gently, softly.*

*Sit with us and create a stillness
known only in small, empty chapels at sundown.
Be there with us
as our witness and as our friend.
Please do not give us advice, suggestions, comparisons
        or another appointment. (That is for later.)*

*We want only a quiet shoulder upon which to rest our
        heads.
If you cannot give us back our sweet dream
then comfort us through this evening.
Hold us. Rock us until morning light creeps in.
Then we will rise and begin the work of a new day.*

Having a child with a significant disability is not easy; it is never what one asks for as a parent, rarely what one expects. Janice and her husband, Rich Feldman, committed themselves to making Micah's life as typical as possible. They pushed actively for his inclusion in public school and in regular classes. Real belonging comes from being *with* other children, and not by being educated *near* them. Micah describes his own journey as follows:

Inclusive education

I have a cognitive impairment, but I have been in inclusive education for my entire school life. In grade one, I was in a special education classroom, but I told my parents: "I want to go in the same door as my friends." They helped me to do that, and from then on I was in an inclusive classroom. I was the first student in Berkley Public Schools to be fully included from elementary through high school.

In high school, I learned other ways of doing things. Because of my disability, I don't write, and reading is difficult for me. I learned to use a computer, and in my senior year I started using a special program called Dragon Speak. This program lets me talk into the computer, and it will type what I say. I have screen reader software that will read whatever is on the computer screen to me—even websites and emails. I was a part of all my meetings, including my IEPs. My friends also were a part of the planning meetings and would talk about my strengths. I used Power Points in my meetings to tell the team about my plans, my strengths, and my dreams.

While I was in high school, I got involved in sports. I was on the cross country and the track team. One of my biggest accomplishments was getting a varsity letter in cross country during my senior year of high school, when I ran a two-mile run in 23 minutes.

Going to college

In my senior year of high school, all of my friends were talking about college. I would hear them say things like: "I got into the University of Michigan." I realized that I wanted to be able to say that I got into college, too. I thought it would be a cool experience to be a college student. Last year, a new program started at Oakland University in Rochester, Michigan, for people with developmental disabilities. It was started by a few very caring people who thought outside the box. They are my parents, teachers, university people, and me. It's called Oakland University Transition.

My first day of college was a bit scary, but I got used to it. Overall, the transition was fun and exciting, and I had a good teacher who helped me make my dream to go to college come true. I take two buses to the campus and sometimes get a ride home with a friend. In the Oakland University Transition program, students like me take two to four classes and do volunteer job training exercises at the Lowry Childhood Education Center and the student radio station WXOU. I also work at the Student Activities Center. We're also involved in the recreation and social stuff on campus. I still have an IEP, and I have meetings at the end of every year, just like I did in high school.

Helpful peers

This semester, I'm taking a communication class and a mental health class, and I'm taking an independent study on computers. I get help from my peers, and I get help from the teachers in my program. My peer helpers will send me emails, or help me to make flash cards and talk to me on the phone. I can meet with the professors and go over notes with them, too. When I take tests and exams, someone reads them to me.

I also get to complete assignments in different ways. For example, in one class I had, all the students had to write a paper about the Bush versus Kerry election, and the teacher asked me if I wanted to do a videotape instead. So I did an interview with Elizabeth Bauer of the Michigan State Board of Education about her job and stuff.

The best part of being at college is being around my peers. I don't have to be with kids who are younger than me. I can be with people who are 20, like me, and hang out with them and have fun.

Being part of the community

In addition to my school work, I do a lot of extracurricular stuff. I am in the Social Work club at the college and in Hillel, a Jewish club. I'm in another Jewish group outside school, called USY (United Synagogue Youth). I'm also on the national youth board of KASA, which stands for Kids As Self Advocates. It's a branch of an organization called Family Voices.

I joined the board of KASA in 2001.[48]

Self-advocacy

I think self-advocacy is really important, because if you don't advocate you don't get what you want. The way I self-advocate is by telling people what I want and what I need.

My advice to other kids with disabilities is to talk to other people. Talk to your parents and to your teachers. If you want to go to college, it's up to you to make a good life for yourself!

It is easy to read Micah's story and realize how wonderful and powerful inclusion has been for *him*. But what about the other students in his classes? Did his inclusion slow them down? Impede their learning? Limit their future options because they spent time with him?

Two of Micah's friends, Matt and Mike, offer powerful testimony of why inclusion matters for students who *don't* have disabilities and of how it transforms the very nature of schooling and community. Matt and Mike have both joined Micah in speaking at inclusion conferences, and they have offered their perspectives to those audiences and for this book.

Mike Boyd writes:

I met Micah in the first grade, and that day we met will stick out in my mind for the rest of my life. You see, my desk was kitty-corner to Micah's, and Katie's (still one of my best friends today) was right next to his.

One day we were all sitting there at our desks, and Micah got sick, real sick. It ended up on his desk, my desk, Katie's desk, and so on; I think you get the point. Just about every single person in the class starting laughing and saying "sick, ughh," but I didn't. At that time I had absolutely no clue who Micah was, but that was not the point. I didn't know Micah had what some may call a learning disability or wasn't able to read or write like most of us were learning, to me he was just like everyone else. To this day I feel the exact same way, he is just like everyone else... different....

No, Micah can't read as fast as you can, but when you read something to Micah he will remember it better than you will. That is what I wanted to explain my whole entire life to people who look differently at Micah. They see this kid, and some just don't want to give him a chance, but Micah has made me want to succeed. My whole life he has looked up to me, envied me, acted like me, and in no way could I ever let him down.

After 1st grade we didn't really meet again until 3rd grade when Circle of Friends[49] was started. Circle of Friends was an after school program created to give students an opportunity to interact with Micah.... Each year a different group, but each year the same idea, fun. We did many things such as community service, local news broadcasts, sports events, and so on. We met at least one time a week after school to discuss with the school social worker things we felt Micah was doing good with and things we felt he needed to work on. After the talk we went on to eat, play, and have fun with one another.... I have always felt if we are to hide the real world events and situations that many kids growing up experience from Micah, are we really doing something good?...

Most likely if and when I get married, Micah will be standing up there with me. He has been one of few that have proven to me that he is a lifetime friend. He calls me all the time and we talk baseball, school, politics and just about anything that comes to mind.... I have been blessed to have known him for this long, and I will only continue to benefit throughout our lives together.

From his relationship with Micah, Mike learned to see people as they really are, to reach beyond superficial images and labels.

Another friend, Matt Weinger, writes about the ways in which the Circle of Friends, developed to surround Micah, ended up surrounding him as a new student as well.

I moved to suburban Detroit from out of state toward the end of fifth grade, when I was ten years old. I found myself as the much maligned "new kid" amongst seventy-five or so children who'd been together since kindergarten. What easily could have meant disaster for my self-esteem instead became a love affair with my new "friends." I was almost immediately embraced, welcomed and included by Micah and his peers, a group known as the "Circle of Friends."

It turns out that being the "new kid" is a blessing in disguise. I'm sure Micah at the time thought very little of what he had done. But look, that's the whole point! To him I was merely a new friend. A quick display of friendliness and compassion on his part meant the entire world to someone else, that being me. I won't ever forget that day. . . . Circle of Friends more than opened my eyes; it opened my heart and opened my mind.

I no longer see the world the way I used to see it. No more "cool kids & weirdoes" or "jocks & dorks." No more "retards." Micah, his family and his circle have taught me to view and accept people as individuals without classifications. Just because someone stutters doesn't mean they aren't worthy of conversation. A blind man would certainly enjoy being read aloud to. Someone who can't run so fast may still get satisfaction from being a member of a track and field team. A child who has poor penmanship could well be a magnificent writer. Luckily, the standards by which society measures people are evolving, if ever for the better. . . .

Thanks to Micah and his Circle of Friends, I feel as though I'm a better friend, a better person, leading a better life.

As articulated in the vision section, inclusion not only allows students to learn compassion, perspective taking, and responsibility, it also shifts their understanding of their own agency and importance in making the world different. Inclusion is about creating schools that are learning communities in which all members are treated with kindness and respect. Though this goal may be achievable without the presence of students with disabilities, the authenticity of thinking about a real student in a real school moves inclusive thinking and a positive response to diversity from a theory to a concrete set of practices. Making a school better for some students can help us think about how to make positive changes for more students. Although Mike Weinger did *not* have a disability, the presence of a welcoming community, a circle of friends constructed to support Micah, drew him into a web of acceptance as well.

Mike's mother, Jan Boyd, describes how Micah's Circle of Friends promoted the inclusion of other children as well.

I am reminded of an incident during this school year when a new student arrived and was not only new to the district, but also new to the culture of the United States, having lived in a different country prior to moving here. The Circle befriended him and asked him to join their meetings and activities. It was this group of youth that helped him feel welcomed in a new environment. This was a wonderful example of taking the term "special needs" to a new dimension. For I think that these young people don't only associate the word "special needs" with a particular disability, but they have a clear understanding that there are many forms of special needs that need to be addressed and nurtured. What a beautiful lesson for each and every one of us.

Another of Micah's friends, Oliver Hersey, gives evidence that the teachings of inclusion continue to shape the lives, choices, and careers of the students who were Micah's peers. Oliver writes:

When I was a second semester senior in high school, I was definitely ready to move on to life AFTER high school. I was ready to be out. When the school social worker asked me if I wanted to earn a half-credit by being a peer tutor for a tenth grader who had a cognitive disability and was included in the general education science class, I gladly accepted. Truthfully I wanted to "blow off" class, and this definitely sounded like a great option.

My responsibilities were to assist Micah in reading

and writing. It took some time for me to understand exactly what that meant. When I would read from the textbook, he would get bored easily, and his eyes would wander out the window. As time went on, I realized that Micah was not really absorbing much of the material. He needed something else to stimulate his mind. Thus, I began using real life examples and talking about science and how it relates to our everyday life. If we were talking about velocity in science class, I talked about the speeding cars in the school parking lot. If we were talking about solids, liquid, and gas, we went to the drinking fountain and let water run over our hands. Micah began to understand the basic concepts of science as we know them today. As time went on I realized that I was not just teaching Micah, but rather Micah was also teaching me. Micah was challenging me to learn about him and the ways he comprehended the material.

Although my sole focus in the beginning of the semester was to assist Micah in science class, I began to learn about Micah as a person. We began to spend time together outside of class. I began learning that Micah had the same needs as me and that we shared a lot in common, especially sports (Go Pistons!). This might sound strange, but I believe that when kids with disabilities are not included and actively participating in school, "general-ed students" never learn how to develop relationships with them. You get a very narrow picture of who they are. They are just the "spec ed" kids. They are just labels—someone you might say "hi" to, but that's about it.

Being with Micah opened my eyes and I guess my heart too. I now know how important it is to get to know the person. To start from a place that recognizes that all human beings share the desire to have friends and "hang out." I learned that you can only become friends over time, over conversation, and being involved in real activities.

To this day Micah and I are friends. We talk regularly and hang out together. In June 2005, he danced at my wedding, and most recently he flew on his own to visit me in Chicago. We will be friends for life. Micah has had a huge impact on me. When it was time to write my final paper during my senior year in college describing my approach and philosophy on teaching, nearly 30% of the content was about what I had learned from my relationship with Micah. He taught me that every student learns at a different pace. That students aren't just in school to get an education but also there to develop social skills and lifelong friends. He challenged me to teach everyone as much as I can.

Now I am a first-year teacher in the Chicago area. I continue to practice what I learned about inclusion and friendships. There is a photo of Micah with his big smile in my classroom reminding me of what true friendship is and how important it is that every student in my classroom feels included. There is a young man with Asperger's syndrome who is a student in my classroom. Although his needs are different than Micah's, I often try to get him involved with the other students in ways that he might not do himself.

I believe that inclusion is a powerful tool that when

used properly has a lifelong effect. I first learned it when I was a student in high school sitting next to Micah in science class. I am now learning it as a teacher in high school.

Micah's sister, Emma Fialka-Feldman, has also become a strong advocate for social justice—a powerful voice for kindness and respect. These are lessons she learned by being Micah's sister—and from witnessing the gap between schools as they are and how she envisions they should and could be.

The following is part of a letter that Emma wrote, at age fourteen, to the teachers and staff in her (and Micah's) school. Her strong voice is evidence of one of the important lessons of inclusion: courage.

Every day when I get up to go to school—I get a little afraid. I am not afraid of the teachers or any particular students. For the most part I like most of the people in my school. But there is one thing that happens every day that disturbs me. When I walk out of a classroom and step out of doorway I cross my fingers hoping I won't hear a student call someone a "retard." Because every time I do, a sharp pain goes through my chest.

My brother Micah, 20, has a cognitive impairment. Every time I hear the r-word I get the chills and become upset. It's not because I think that the student using the r-word is referring to my brother, because they probably aren't, but because they've learned that it is acceptable to use that word. The problem is that it is NOT okay to call someone a retard. Just like society has learned that an African American should no longer be called a "nigger," because it is a derogatory word, now it is time to learn that no one should be called a retard.

Every time I hear someone use the r-word, I have to make a decision. Do I walk up to the student and say, "That's unacceptable, you know, to use that word." The person usually stands there trying to recall their words. I stand there wondering why I have to be the one telling them this. Then I continue. "I hope you stop using the r-word because—just like you would probably never call someone the n-word—you shouldn't call someone a retard. It is unacceptable." Or do I not say anything because I am too tired of saying it?

At a camp I attended this summer, one camper constantly used the r-word. Not being able to stand it any longer, I finally asked him to stop. His response was so powerful that it forced me to write this letter to you. He said, "Retard is the only word I can get away with at my school." I was shocked and appalled. But I had no reason to be. In my 10 years at Berkley—I've only known ONE teacher who has ever said anything to a student, in front of me, when the r-word was used. Granted there are probably teachers who may have heard a student using the r-word and pulled them aside and told them to stop. I commend all of you who have done that. Unfortunately there haven't been enough teachers and staff doing it especially in front of the classroom, the hallways, or during conversations. A child shouldn't be able to know they can get away with using a derogatory word in their school.

Maybe there will be a day when I'll walk down the

hallways of BHS and I won't be scared because I'll know that there's a group of people, not only teachers, but also my fellow classmates, who have learned to accept each other's differences and use respectful language. Maybe then there will be no sharp pains through my heart, only a satisfied smile.

Civil rights, the importance of our language, the role of allies in challenging oppression—these are not abstract concepts to Emma and her friends. Rather, they understand social justice at a deep, intimate level—it is part of their lives and will undoubtedly follow them into their future lives, regardless of their journeys or careers.

It is important to emphasize that this inclusion process didn't just *happen*. Rather, it was the result of the effort, commitment, and vigilance of many people, including Micah's parents and school staff.

Micah's mother and father worked continuously to negotiate the system for their son: how much should they push for Micah's inclusion? If they didn't push, would it all unfold naturally? How much priming does the system need?

In an article titled "Nudging the Network," Janice describes how many well-intentioned efforts to include Micah simply didn't work. Although a basketball coach tried to engineer a successful moment by adding Micah to the fifth-grade basketball team's play for the last three minutes of the game, Micah had never developed enough basketball skills to make that happen. Inclusion can't be about programming a few moments of "inclusion success," photo opportunities of inclusive practice, but about committing for the long haul, constantly assessing the learning environment and figuring out how it can be expanded, shaped, prodded, and molded to be more inclusive.

She writes:

> Although far from easy, we have learned to hold conversations and meetings where we have explicitly asked the question, "What can we all do to ensure that Micah has a role in the action, an assignment, a part of the play, a ride to the dance, a meaningful way to be?" We've learned that young people have great ideas.
>
> We've learned that it's okay—in fact, necessary to nudge his network a bit. For example, one of Micah's personal goals for his senior year was to go to the prom. After little success hoping that he'd get a date or be invited to join one of the groups, we decided to "nudge his network"; that is, to make contact with the Circle of Friends. It wasn't easy to hear the "I-already-have-plans-sorry..." response, but we didn't give up. Micah made some calls, but time was running out. Soon we connected with one of our newest recruits to the Circle, Shosh. She had won our hearts when we saw her running on the same cross country team with Micah. She wanted to include Micah in her group going to the prom, but there were the other 13 kids in her group who needed to be consulted. Can you imagine trying to consult with 13 teens and get consensus? The phone lines were hot.
>
> Eight days passed, each involving many, many phone calls—but it worked out well for everyone. Micah was joining the group of 14 kids going to his senior prom—the most important dream of his se-

nior year. Later a sweet and unexpected call came from Michael, one of Micah's longest friends. "Hey Micah, wanna go shopping for our tuxedos?"

Micah's parents learned that inclusion doesn't just happen. It takes hard work, thoughtful planning, trial and error, and lots of persistence.

It took tremendous and collaborative problem solving, but Micah *did* go to the prom. And although he never did score a basket in a basketball game, Micah went on to run cross country and track, eventually leading to a varsity letter. And finally, without parental involvement, Micah was elected to the Homecoming Court in his senior year! Sweet success. Powerful inclusion. Important lessons for everyone involved.

Micah's story is not typical, but neither is it rare. Micah's father describes the process as "a journey and not a miracle" with many sad and frustrating days, in addition to those of joy. But knowing this happened for this young man helps us see the possibilities for others. How do we make this occur for all students? How do we reorganize classrooms and schools so that inclusion is the norm and not the exception? The next chapter addresses the critical steps of getting started with inclusion and making it successful.

Three: Getting It Right/ Doing It Well

6. Building Inclusive Classroom Communities

Many things have to be in place to make an inclusion system work smoothly and effectively. In this chapter, I draw on the voices and experiences of real teachers and students who are making inclusion a practical reality. I present glimpses of inclusive classrooms that demonstrate the principles I have articulated. And I ask you to think about the ways in which these changes benefit a broad range of students—and all of us.

Inclusion calls into question many aspects of the traditional classroom and pushes them to change in many ways. We have to rethink how we help children to interact and talk about one another, we have to envision curricula and pedagogy that work for all learners, and we have to link our inclusive classrooms to broader school and societal visions.

I begin this chapter with the organizing concept of building community in the classroom. Though all classrooms benefit from a sense of community and connection among students, teachers, and staff, inclusive classrooms demand attention to community from the beginning and throughout every aspect of the school day.

Without a strong community, inclusion cannot work. The perils of not paying close attention to community building is evident in the literature, which is full of stories of students whose "inclusion" meant only that their bodies were near those of more typical students. These children had little interaction with classmates, no friendships, and very minimal participation.

Eugene Marcus, a man with autism, was one such student. When I asked him to talk about his inclusion experience, he wrote: "I was only partly included. My body was there, but so was the class gerbil. Unless inclusion is about everyone participating, it doesn't really count."

Such classrooms, which move bodies into shared space and call it "inclusion," are set up for failure, and they miss the educational, social, and motivational power of inclusive classrooms. In order for inclusion to be successful, all students need to be full members of their classroom and school communities.

But how do we get there? What does it mean for a classroom or a school to be a community of learners? What would it look like? How would it feel?

Most of us have memories of times and places in which we have felt truly known, accepted, and valued. Perhaps it was a youth group that worked together to clean up after a storm, an orchestra or choral group that worked hard to produce a satisfying performance, or a community that gathered to support a family or individual in need.

There are many kinds of communities. Some are intentional: a group of people decide to live, work or play together. Other communities evolve by chance when people find themselves working on the same project. Long-lived or temporary, all communities can be powerful.

People sometimes describe a good classroom community as a family. But for many people, the word "family" does not evoke warmth, security, and love; that wasn't their personal experience of family. But it *is* possible to articulate the way we would *like* our "family" to feel. Some of us, who live either far away or are otherwise removed from our families of origin, have created families of choice.

Every Thursday night, I have dinner with a family that has been carefully and lovingly constructed. My own children no longer live at home, but my "new" family includes Emmi, who is nine, and Eli, who just turned three. Although they have no biological connection, Eli calls Emmi his "big sister," and Emmi refers to my daughters as her "big sisters." This new family is created through intention and routines. We choose to be together, we commit to making it happen consistently, and we engage in sharing and communication that deepen our connections. We begin dinner by holding hands in a circle, this silence often punctuated by childish laughter or by Eli piping in "We're closing our eyes now. I have my eyes closed. I'm opening my eyes." We try to breathe into the moment, honoring the importance of our coming together.

We spend dinnertime "checking in" with each other, sharing the high points and low points of our week. Who has been ill? Who's better? What's happened at school? At work? Who has news or an accomplishment to share? Eli is making real progress on getting toilet-trained! Emmi can do a back walkover in her gymnastics class; Cheri saved the life of a sick rabbit in her veterinary practice; Mayer taught a great seminar to teachers; Barb had an article accepted for publication; Steve's wrist is getting better after his surgery; Andy's political work with the local Native American community is going well; Annegret is excitedly planning her summer visit to Germany to see her family. Dinnertime is full of stories, laughter, occasional tears, gestures of sympathy, reassurances, promises of support, expressions of gratitude, future plans, and lots of talking.

It is not difficult to imagine how one builds community among friends and neighbors—people we see consistently and with whom we form relationships. But is it possible to make the school classroom feel like a community? The challenges of school policies and practices (like competition and grading, tracking and segregation) that impede relationship building and a sense of safety are real—but they can be overcome.

Community building, like inclusion, is intentional and requires ongoing focus and commitment. It's not something enacted for the first week of school before going on to the "real" work of learning. Community building is thoroughly integrated into everything that happens in the classroom—it is inextricably linked to the other learning in the classroom. Community building is about how adults talk to students, it's about what's on the walls, the books we read, and the songs we sing. And it's about what happens when something goes wrong in class. Building community *is* a real lesson in itself.

At Solace Elementary School in Syracuse, New York, every school morning begins with a schoolwide assembly. Students sing together, teachers and students announce individual and group accomplishments, students read stories and poems they've written, and schoolwide issues and concerns are addressed. Students feel that they are part of a school community, not just a grade-level classroom. The school is small enough for everyone to know everyone else. When one of the third graders was getting teased because she had two dads, the issue was openly and directly addressed; one of the girl's fathers came and talked to the class about their family, about the difference between appropriate and intrusive questions, and about the need for kindness and understanding.

Community building centers on two things: establishing (proactively) norms of community and responding thoughtfully to challenges to that sense of community. Community building requires thinking—*before* the name calling, the conflict on the playground, or the formation of cliques—about what the culture of the classroom will be and how these norms will be established with students. Rule setting goes beyond how many students can use the drinking fountain or sharpen their pencils and includes explicit discussions of how we treat one another. Will name calling be allowed? Will children be allowed to exclude others from their play or work? Will classmates be encouraged to help one another, or will any attempts at interpersonal communication be labeled "off task" and "cheating"?

In one school I visited recently, the class had only one rule: "We don't hurt each other's insides or outsides." There was no need for pages of details—the core values were clear, and they were communicated explicitly.

What are the components of a community, and how do we develop them within our schools and classrooms? Below, I will present some key aspects of community that contribute to a sense of connectedness and cohesiveness, components that must be present for inclusion to work. These include safety, open communication, and norms of inclusion and cooperation.

SAFETY

A community should feel safe. It should be physically safe—no one would hit you or hurt you—and emotionally safe as well. In such a community, no one would call you names, call attention to your failures, or compare you negatively to themselves or others. A nurturing community is a place where it is safe to be yourself. Most significant, with reference to inclusion, it is safe to be yourself as you are *right now*. We don't welcome you now because of what you may become; you do not have to "earn" your right to be in the community. You simply belong because you are here. This is an attitude of unconditional acceptance.

In a safe classroom, Garret can say that he doesn't understand math and receive help and support rather than scorn or derision. Ashanti can display the painting she made and receive appreciation and praise, rather than envy or indifference. We learn about one another's challenges and weaknesses so we can help each other, not so we can make fun of each other. We become tender and supportive when we know someone is vulnerable and hurting. We learn to reach out with hugs and kind words, with tissues and reassurance.

In one inclusive classroom I visited recently, one of the second graders cried every morning when his mother left. Although it was well into the school year, the teacher encouraged Dominic's classmates to bring him tissues and remind him that he'd be okay. There was no teasing, no humiliation, or chiding, no cajoling him to "grow up and act like a big boy." The students learned compassion from their teacher—and they learned that everyone is different. Many of them didn't exactly understand Dominic's tears as it didn't reflect most of their own feelings or experiences, but they could relate their own challenges to the one they were observing and figure out how to be supportive.

Cathi Allen, a third-grade teacher in Bountiful, Utah, has frequent class meetings and uses five key agreements with the students to promote safety and positive interaction. The rules focus on appreciation, mutual respect, attentive listening, honoring confidentiality, and the right to pass on your turn. Revisiting these rules allows her students to openly discuss what *they* need to feel safe in her room.

In a safe classroom community, the teacher and other

school staff are also able to be themselves, sometimes accomplished and sometimes struggling. I watched with great satisfaction in one classroom as the teacher acknowledged her own problems with spelling to the students, who were then eager to help her by looking up words, becoming her human spellcheckers. I observed the amazing effects on community when a teacher shared her sadness at a recent miscarriage and her hope to someday be a mother. Safe communities let us breathe deeply—our place assured.

OPEN COMMUNICATION

In an inclusive community, students talk about who they are, how they are the same, how they are different, and what they need from friends and classmates. When students notice that Caitlin's eyes are almond-shaped, they discuss her adoption from Korea and her plans to go to Korean Culture Camp this summer to learn more about her heritage. Students openly discuss Jason's anger on the playground at recess and what they can do to make sure that he feels included in games and activities. Classmates discuss what they will do to make sure Jarred, who uses a wheelchair, can be part of the upcoming school play. The name-calling that is happening on the playground and what to do about it are openly discussed.

Anne Dobbelaere, a kindergarten teacher in a very inclusive school, explains children's differences with accuracy without stigma or embarrassing language. She says, of a child who still wets his pants, "George is learning how to get to the bathroom in time." She says of a child with autism whose anger sometimes erupts in circle time, "Margaret is learning how to use her words when she's angry instead of pulling people's hair." I watch with wonder as she teaches the other children how to gently grasp Margaret's hand when she pulls their hair in order to release her grip. I hear them say, "Margaret, I know you're angry. But you can't pull my hair. Do you want to sit next to me?" Anne uses language that helps students understand one another and that encourages them to support one another. She doesn't make students with disabilities the "other"—she doesn't label Margaret as autistic or imply that George is to blame for his wetting accidents. She helps the children to understand that just as some of them are learning to tie their shoes, recite the alphabet, or master holding a pencil, George and Margaret are also learning things.

Not only is there honesty about what is going on in the classroom and about individual students' challenges and accomplishments, but there is also space and respect for multiple forms of communication.

The nonverbal student who uses assistive technology, painstakingly pointing to each letter she wants to communicate, is acknowledged as having something to say. Students learn to be patient with those whose speech or communication is slow or awkward. Students in inclusive classrooms know that not being able to talk or talk well has nothing to do with intelligence. Multiple languages are honored, and the goal is a measure of multilingualism for *all* students; hearing students learn some sign language, and there are sincere attempts to teach all students at least a little of the Spanish and other languages represented in the community; careful attention is paid to understanding body language and alternative ways of expressing feelings and ideas.

Jamie Burke, a young man with autism, types an answer to the question "What would a school of your dreams look like?":

A school of good soft seats and desks that held wonderful books that told of love and kindness to each other. Kids would need to behave in a most kind manner and teasing would be a detention time. Everyone would be asked to join all clubs if desired and pleasing music would play everywhere.... My school is very good and people try both teaching and loving me and my autism. Respect comes with love and understanding each kid's abilities... so therefore teachers must have a desire to teach everyone.... Conversations with me will tell you if I am happy.[50]

What powerful lessons do students (and adults) learn by finding out that the young woman who flaps her arms and makes startling noises is actually someone who is thinking and feeling about school—often very much as they do?

NORMS OF INCLUSION

Inclusive communities need explicit norms of including others. These messages are sent implicitly as well. The teacher who lines students up by gender or who places students' desks apart from others is communicating powerful messages about students' connections and responsibilities to one another.

Popular media can easily distort our classroom values if we are not vigilant. In one third grade I visited recently, the teacher, as if taking cues from the TV show *Survivor,* asked students in each row to "vote a student off the row" each week. Students got to choose who would be eliminated from their classroom community and asked to sit in a separate section of the classroom. I can only wonder and worry about what criteria the students used to eliminate one another. The effects on community were immediate and powerful—the creation of a two-tiered classroom made up of "community members" and "noncommunity members," as they were called.

It is not enough to simply "be" inclusive—it must be something we discuss, understand, and make visible in our interactions. One preschool teacher taught her three-year-old students to tell the difference between words that "bring us together" and words that "push us apart." By establishing this terminology, she was able to help children look at what they said and heard. She could ask, "Does telling Lydia, 'We don't want to play with you' bring us together or push us apart?"

Vivian Paley's landmark book *You Can't Say You Can't Play* (discussed in chapter 2) was at the heart of an action research project in which I collaborated with four inclusive classroom teachers.[51] All four teachers taught at Ed Smith Elementary School in Syracuse, New York, a K-6 school of approximately eight hundred students in thirty-five classrooms. The school is well known for its efforts and success at implementing full inclusion, and a significant number of students with disabilities are enrolled there, testimony to the ways in which the school has attracted parents seeking inclusion. The four teachers, Anne Dobbelaere (kindergarten), Mary C. Mastin (first grade), Kathy Goodman (second grade), and Cathleen Corrigan (fourth grade), were all already committed to full inclusion. Nonetheless, they were eager to explore how altering the social climate of their classrooms might increase the inclusion of students with disabilities and other students who tended to be left out or isolated.

The project involved reading the book together, discussing our own experiences with exclusion in our lives, exploring the ethical and logistical implications of attempting to influence social interaction in the classroom, and then, finally, the implementation of the rule—"You can't say, 'You can't play' "—in each classroom.

During the first year of the project, two observers collected field notes on students' social relationships and the effects of the rule's implementation. The research team (the four teachers and I) met regularly to discuss what the observers and teachers had seen and to discuss our responses and feelings. At the end of the year, I interviewed students at each grade level to learn their perspectives on the social climate in their rooms and their perceptions of the effects of the rule.

As might be expected, and as Paley's own experience bears out, the results of the rule's implementation varied not only across classes but also across grade levels. The developmental and conceptual understandings of kindergartners and fourth graders varied, as did the ways the teachers implemented the rule, talked to students, and engaged them in problem solving.

Kindergarten teacher Anne Dobbelaere found that her students quickly accepted the rule, but she spent a lot of time helping students figure out *how* to include one another. Her students role-played asking each other to play and entering already established groups. First-grade teacher Mary Mastin (and her teaching partner, Lois Eddy) realized that implementing the rule meant changing the rules for how students were limited at the daily learning centers. The new rule explicitly allowed many children to be in the same center at the same time. After a brief flurry of confusion ("Can we really go anywhere we want to?"), Mary reported that the rule directly affected friendship and interaction patterns: "It worked out really well. Some kids previously wouldn't go into an area unless their friends could go with them. When we took the limit off, the groups of kids that interacted were more varied. They could be with their friends, but also with other kids, so they had more interactions."

My interviews with the first graders reinforced what their teachers saw. One girl told me, "It changed things for the good because some people didn't play with other kids. Sometimes, they didn't play with kids who wanted to play with them.... Now, the kids are finding out that they can have real fun with the other kids that they weren't playing with before."

The students perceived that the rule had changed the number of people who now played together, the variety of people who played together, and the ways in which they talked to one another and played together.

After some initial frustration because of the number of children who tattled and the complexities of supporting impulsive children in learning to manage their feelings, second-grade teacher Kathy Goodman reported that their persistence paid off. "Surprisingly, the effects of implementing the rule had at least as much influence on me as on the children. It challenged us all to work hard creating and maintaining a more idealistic world. Ultimately, most children responded on some level to the absolute fairness of the rule. At the end of the year, I had to admit I'd never seen a group of kids change so dramatically. I had grown, too."

Like the older students in Paley's book, the fourth graders were more reluctant to embrace the rule wholeheartedly. They already had established "clubs" and cliques (one club even had its own newspaper), and their friendship patterns were well ingrained. But Cathleen Corrigan persisted, encouraging students to journal about whether the rule was "fair" and whether it was "working." The students overwhelmingly said that the rule was fair, even if they didn't *like* it.

But the turning point came on the playground. Because students from various classes have recess together, Cathleen's fourth graders were with other students on the playground. When one of her students was told that he couldn't join the soccer game because "Our class doesn't have that stupid rule," Cathleen's students were enraged. They returned to the class eager to talk about what they should do, including talking to other teachers about the rule and the importance of making it a "school rule" and not just one for their classroom. They discussed what they would do when they went on to fifth grade and why they thought the rule was a good idea. These students had a clear understanding of the difference between piecemeal change and systemic, structural reform.

My interviews with the fourth graders were revealing. Students reported that they no longer reflexively said *No* when someone asked to join them. They explained how they negotiated letting people in—waiting for turns, finding appropriate entry moments. One boy explained, "Well, we don't always let people play. But we talk about it a lot more!" It was almost as if the rule gave students permission to be their nicer selves —they had the force of the rule behind them to be inclusive, and they were less subject to peer pressure to exclude.

The "You can't say, 'You can't play' " rule raised issues of inclusion and exclusion to an unprecedented level of saliency and visibility in the classroom. Students didn't just talk about math or reading or social studies; now they *also* talked about how people were being treated in the classroom, their struggles with letting people play who behaved inappropriately and how to include a child with a significant disability in their game.

Clearly the rule is not a panacea. Nor is it something to put on the wall and hope for the best. But in the hands of teachers who were seriously committed to structuring positive social interactions and who were already committed to inclusion, the rule was the beginning of powerful discussions. For the students with disabilities, the rule was not sufficient, because it permitted a form of passive exclusion. That is, if the person didn't ask to play, he didn't have to be included. For the rule to work, all students had to be able to initiate invitations to those who didn't or couldn't ask to join. Students with disabilities may need direct instruction on how to initiate play, and "typical" students may need to become skilled in noticing the child on the periphery, able and willing to ask, "Do you want to play with us?"

George Theoharis, principal of Falk School in Madison, Wisconsin, extended the principles of inclusion beyond individual classrooms. As in many schools, the playground was the site of much exclusion—those who didn't bring equipment from home had nothing to play with, students wandered around aimlessly, and fights broke out about how games were *supposed* to be played. He and his staff implemented a playground program that involved spending several weeks using physical education classes to teach all students games, and they established a set of rules. Theoharis used a minigrant to buy playground equipment so that all balls, bats, and ropes belonged to the school, which prevented students from bringing individual equipment and then reclaiming it if the game wasn't going their way. Students, parents, and staff all participated in painting games on the blacktop and staff took turns, at lunchtime, actually running games with students so that there was always something to do. He reported that there were many fewer fights on the playground and that many kids were playing and doing different things. He also implemented an equipment checkout system that was run by the fourth and fifth graders, who then took ownership of the program and felt empowered to enforce norms of cooperation. Each class was responsible, for two weeks a year, for keeping the playground clear—this was not intended to be a punishment but rather another way to help all students feel that the playground belonged to *them* and was worth keeping nice.

Responsive Classroom is an approach to creating safe, challenging, and joyful elementary schools.[52] The organization offers training for school personnel as well as a host of materials. An article on the Responsive Classroom Web site, titled "Including Wyatt: How Responsive Classrooms Strategies Supported a Child with Special Needs" by Nancy Kovacic, makes clear the connections between a healthy, supportive classroom environment and successful inclusion. The author, a third-grade teacher in Westport, Connecticut, describes the inclusion of Wyatt, a bright and cheerful third grader with cerebral palsy. She details how three aspects of her Responsive Classroom practices all help Wyatt to be fully included. During Morning Meeting, which includes greeting, sharing, a group activity, and news and announcements, Wyatt is a full participant through the use of his DynaVox, which plays recorded phrases aloud when Wyatt presses a control with his headpiece. The teacher and the students have together figured out how Wyatt can participate by signaling his intentions through his locked gaze and by indicating choices on his assistive technology device.

The component of the day titled "academic choice" offers students options about what to learn or how to reach their lesson goals. Because all students are offered options, Wyatt is able to choose those that make sense for him without singling himself out for differential treatment.

The Responsive Classroom approach to discipline, which

stresses including all children in rule creation and generating logical consequences for violations, allows the teachers to help Wyatt make choices about how he fits into the learning community and what is required of him in the classroom. Through the use of a strategy by which students separate themselves from a negative situation to regain their self-control, Wyatt is learning important lessons about his role as a class member and the ways in which his behavior affects others—he is learning empathy. The "typical" children are also able to see that Wyatt is working on the same things that they are and that they are all co-participants in a community-building process.

COOPERATION (NOT COMPETITION)

As mentioned earlier, competition and inclusion are fundamentally incompatible. How can we embrace diversity as a positive, desirable aspect of our classrooms and schools, purposefully make our classrooms inclusive of children who vary in many ways, and then encourage children to compete with one another, ranking and sorting them into winners and losers? How can we say, "It's okay to be different" and then "We will position you so that you can't all be successful"? Inclusion demands establishing classroom norms of cooperation and mutual support. Some of the details about how this can be done relative to curriculum and teaching will be explored in the next chapter. Here we can discuss what classrooms and schools look like when cooperation is one of the core values.

Thinking critically about competition is challenging for many of us. Many of us experienced school as a competitive arena, and, especially for those of us who did well, it's hard to see the problem. We have all been inundated with so many myths about competition (it's motivating, it's the only way to promote high achievement, it builds character) that we often haven't thought deeply about what competition did to our own sense of self and our relationships with others.

When I ask people to reflect on their own experiences with competition in school, there are often stories of pain and isolation for both the winners and the losers. Students who were continually the lowest student in the math class, the poorest reader, or the last chosen for team sports report humiliation and embarrassment. Many adults report giving up activities because they were made to feel inadequate or unsuccessful: I can't sing, I'm not good at sports, I can't draw, I'm bad at math.

But even those people who were the winners often tell about the high price they paid for their success: feelings of isolation, resentment, anger, and alienation from others. Some felt that they had to actively choose between "doing well" and "having friends," a terrible choice to make, and one which, at middle school—when relationships matter so much—often results in plunging achievement.

Alfie Kohn, in his book *No Contest: The Case against Competition*, says that competition is so pervasive that asking people to reflect on the problems with competition—and its alternatives—is like asking a fish to talk about the water; because it's everywhere, it's hard to acknowledge its existence or how much it affected us.

Nonetheless, reconceptualizing classrooms as cooperative communities is worth doing and directly tied to our success in creating inclusive schools. A cooperative classroom is one in which all members work together to achieve mutual goals. These goals can be academic learning, social problem solving, and conflict resolution.

In inclusive classrooms that welcome, acknowledge, and

name the many ways in which students differ, it makes little sense to impose a competitive structure that creates winners and losers. How does offering a prize to the student who finishes his math first affect the child who is working on a different level of math?

Certainly, it makes sense for teachers (and students) to have an accurate assessment of their own levels of understanding and achievement. Appropriate individualization depends on the teacher's knowing the varying skill levels present in the classroom and designing appropriate modifications and challenges.

The question is, what message is publicly sent? What's important is not to create a classroom culture where children are contrasted and treated differently as a function of competitive assessments. Each student needs to be honored and acknowledged for where she is *now* and challenged to move to the next level. Competitiveness suppresses achievement for many, if not most, kids. Pitting children against one another in public competitive environments not only damages their relationships, but also is not—and research bears this out—as effective a road to achievement as is cooperation.

What happens in a cooperative classroom? And, sometimes equally significantly, what *doesn't* happen?

In cooperative classrooms:

• We see all students' work displayed somewhere in the room (everyone has done *something* good); we don't just see the papers of a few high-achieving students.

• Records about who has accomplished a specific learning task are kept privately; we don't see star charts on the wall that make it obvious who is doing well and who is lagging behind. Because students are doing work at their own levels, comparisons on public charts rarely even have meaning.

• People are appreciated for their individual gifts and talents or for group accomplishments ("Emilio, you are really getting faster at your math facts"). There are not constant comparisons about who is ahead, the best, the fastest.

• Students are encouraged to work together to get things done ("Let's see if we can work together to get the room clean quickly so we have time for an extra chapter of our mystery"). Students aren't asked to compete with one another ("There's a prize for the row that gets its desks cleaned up first").

• Peer support, tutoring, and help are actively encouraged and structured ("Quentin, why don't you ask one of your table-mates to show you how to finish coloring the map?"). Helping one another isn't discouraged by reflexively calling it cheating ("Quinn, I want to know what you can do, not your neighbor—do your own work"). We need to think carefully about when it's okay for students to work together and help one another and when we must insist upon individual, independent work.

• Students play cooperative games in which many levels of skill allow the group to do well. The classroom is not dominated by spelling bees, around the world flashcard competitions and other contests that eliminate most students' participation.

In cooperative classrooms, it is possible for students working at many different levels to all feel successful. There is not a zero-sum game in which only some children can be positively affirmed for their work and their progress.

WHEN NEGATIVE THINGS HAPPEN

The establishment of norms of inclusion and cooperation will likely significantly decrease the occurrences of negative peer interactions. But there will undoubtedly still be moments in which a reactive response will be called for.

One advantage of establishing proactive rules and a positive climate is the ability of the teacher to reference those agreements when undesirable things happen: "Andy, is what you said to Marcus consistent with our rule about using kind words?" "Gabriel, how could you and Samantha decide what to do about the drawing so it's a win-win solution?" It is impossible to refer back to norms and expectations if these have never been articulated.

Having classroom and school community-building practices in place allows us to respond more productively in moments of crisis.[53] After September 11, 2001, for example, teachers who had already established a strong classroom community found themselves better able to respond to the devastating tragedy and all the feelings and responses it provoked. Teachers who already had organized a morning meeting and guidelines for community discussion, those who had started journaling with their students, and schools that had a strong school-parent relationship were able to rally and respond quickly. One elementary teacher who already had a word wall that included the words "prejudice," "discrimination," and "acceptance" was able to refer to those words when discussing the targeting of Arabs in the community and the importance of learning about others before jumping to conclusions. In classrooms that begin with an individual check-in for each student, teachers are more likely to be able to take the temperature of their class's social climate and have ways to respond.

Sometimes, sensitive teachers can predict that various experiences or processes will demand thoughtful responses, and they can lay the groundwork proactively. For example, when one teacher's class was about to visit a home for older people, she engaged them in lengthy lessons on how to introduce themselves, how people's abilities to speak and hear may be impaired with age, how to respond respectfully and thoughtfully, and what it means to treat *all* people with dignity. The teacher's ability to preempt certain kinds of negative behavior was a function of her careful preparation of her students for the experience they were about to have. Inclusion teachers whose classrooms include students with a wide range of skills and abilities have unique opportunities to teach students about individual differences, how and when to help one another, and what it means to be a community.

Of course, when kids (people) get together and are asked to collaborate, even in the most supportive, welcoming environments, conflicts will occur. Children's Creative Response to Conflict Program[54] is a national organization that trains teachers and others in conflict resolution skills. They articulate the following concepts as central to their understanding of conflict:

1. Conflict exists and is part of our everyday lives. We must all learn skills to deal with conflict.

2. We can grow through conflict and through learning how to resolve our disagreements.

3. Conflict is complex, and there is usually more than one answer to a problem. Learning to generate multiple solutions and choose among them is crucial to our learning.

4. We can all learn the skills of conflict resolution, and, with practice, we will get better and better at finding solutions.

5. Feelings matter in this process, and we must learn how to talk about and listen to one another's feelings.

6. How we define a problem relates to how we will solve it. Conceptualizing solutions in terms of win-win rather than win-lose will lead us to more productive responses.

In Kim Rombach's first-grade classroom, there are two "talking chairs" at the front of the room. Students who are having a conflict can ask the teacher if they can go to the chairs, sit down, and talk about their problems. Kim has spent considerable time with the students teaching the steps of conflict resolution, and a reminder of the process (in simple language) is posted prominently above the table.

At the Jowonio School,[55] a very inclusive preschool that includes children of many different races, languages, and abilities/disabilities, when two children get into a conflict, they are asked to hold the Heart-to-Heart box. They respond to the questions on the box:

What are you feeling?

Who are you feeling it about?

What happened?

What do you wish happened?

Can you think of something that you like about the other person?

Students are not abandoned to resolve their problems, but are actively scaffolded by teachers and staff who help them to find the language and solutions they want. Although the current focus on high-stakes testing and rigid curriculum guidelines make devoting attention to learning conflict resolution skills more challenging, such instruction has never been more necessary. In addition to the conflicts that occur in classes, the level of bullying, teasing, and harassment in schools has reached epidemic proportions. And our new technologies have lead to cyber-bullying and attack blogs as well as the in-person verbal, emotional, and physical assaults. A recent report on school climate conducted by GLSEN (the Gay, Lesbian, and Straight Education Network)[56] found that 65 percent of teens have been verbally or physically harassed or assaulted during the past year because of their perceived or actual appearance, gender, sexual orientation, gender expression, race/ethnicity, disability, or religion. Thirty-six percent of teens and 53 percent of secondary teachers say that bullying or harassment is a serious problem at their school. How can we expect students to learn academics if they are worried about walking down the hallway, going out on the playground, or eating in the cafeteria?

Descriptions of specific programs that help students to actively challenge racism, homophobia, and ableism will be described in the last section of the book. It is important to note, however, that bullying and teasing rarely just go away. It is up to teachers to establish safe spaces for students and to enforce norms of kindness and respect.

The children's book *Chrysanthemum*, by Kevin Henkes,[57] provides a powerful example of the importance of the teacher in setting class climate. Chrysanthemum, a mouse, loves her name—until she starts school and is mercilessly teased by her classmates for it. In contrast to the classroom teacher who does little to challenge the teasing, the new music teacher, Mrs. Twinkle, observes what's going on and gently engages the class in a discussion of the situation. She tells the class her own long first name—Delphinium—which also scarcely fits on a name tag. Because the students are enamored of their new teacher, and because the teacher supports Chrysanthemum, they change their perceptions and stop their teasing.

Research has shown that teachers who have classrooms in which children treat one another well are neither laissez-faire ("Oh, well, what can you do, kids will be kids") nor punitive, a response that often simply moves the teasing underground, out of the teacher's sight. The expression "Don't let me catch you doing that again" is often precisely what happens; students don't stop—they simply learn to be cleverer about not getting caught.

There are many excellent programs for helping students learn positive responses to diversity, such as those provided by the Developmental Studies Center in California, Teaching Tolerance, the Fourth R in Canada,[58] and by GLSEN. What these programs all have in common is a strong teacher commitment to noticing what is going on and establishing, proactively, a positive classroom environment and responding consistently and powerfully to unacceptable behaviors.

The heart of successful inclusion is relationships. Thus it makes sense that establishing a positive school climate and environment in which those relationships can flourish is essential to making inclusion work.

DIFFERENT FROM WHOM?

LEARNING TO DISCUSS HUMAN VARIATION

In order to move to more fully inclusive models of thinking and teaching—and in order to think about and create true communities—one of the essential steps is a close examination of our language, particularly our language of difference. How can we change our ways of thinking about and talking about human variation, imbuing "difference" with new meanings—or realizing the hollowness of the concept altogether?

Think about the messages we have learned about same and different. Even the *Sesame Street* song says: "One of these things is not like the other; one of these things doesn't belong…" It's good to be the same; it's bad to be different. It's safer to be the same; it's dangerous to stick out. To be different is not to belong.

At an early point in the movement toward multiculturalism, many people advanced "color blindness" as the goal. The argument was that the best solution to prejudice and racism was treating everyone as "people" with no reference to skin color. I still meet people (and teachers) who say, "I look at my children, and I just don't see color." The underlying assumption was that "seeing," "recognizing," or "naming" color was undesirable, and somehow implied that one was racist or had inbred prejudice toward people of particular colors. Given that belief, it's not surprising that the proposed solution was *not* to see or mention color.

A friend, who is African American and the director of human resources for a large urban school district, reported that at a recent Parent-Teacher Organization meeting, a mother (white) approached her and said: "I'm so proud of my son.

He's been in kindergarten now for three weeks, and he hasn't noticed that his teacher's black." My friend responded with feigned alarm, "Does he have visual problems?"

The reason we can laugh at this anecdote and what it conveys, I think, is that today, there is a wide cultural consensus, in schools and elsewhere, that in the realm of race and ethnicity, the goal of color blindness has proven to be both impossible and undesirable. People do come in an assortment of colors (and sizes and shapes and so on), and we now increasingly recognize that every person has multiple identities. I am a woman, a Jew of European descent, middle-class, currently able-bodied—the list is endless. Each of these identities brings to the table a set of life experiences, beliefs, and attitudes. Some of these identities have been the source of privilege and power in my life (my social class and skin color) and others have been the source of prejudice or discrimination (my religion and my gender). Some have been both.

It is increasingly clear that our goal in education cannot be and should not be to "erase" differences, rendering everyone vaguely "the same," without regard to who each person really is.

Despite this transformation within the area of multiculturalism and diversity, there are still those who argue that success for those with disabilities and for the inclusion process will be achieved when people "don't notice" disabilities. They may claim that a "good inclusive classroom" is one in which "you can't tell who the children with disabilities are." This construct has significant effects on how teachers are prepared and how they respond to the differences in their classrooms.

Responding sensitively to differences is at the heart of inclusive teaching, but how are we to understand and talk about what "difference" means and how we relate to it? Our language is powerful; what we say both reflects and shapes our perceptions.

The children who come to our schools are different from one another and are so in many ways. Alternatively, we could say that they vary in many ways. They have different color skin, they come from different kinds of families, and they speak different languages. Some of them are short, others are tall, some are heavy, others are light, some are athletic, and others struggle with moving through space gracefully. Students vary in their verbal skills, their social skills, their athletic skills, their large and fine motor control, and in their interests. They celebrate different holidays, they eat different foods, and they listen to different music—or to no music at all. The list is endless.

What is challenging, I believe, is that our responses to these variations can take many forms: we can ignore them, we can name them, we can accommodate them, we can celebrate them, we can seek to eliminate them, and we can seek to remediate them. Depending on what particular area of variation we are discussing, the responses may be very different, and they depend on our values, our goals, and our resources.

How do we decide which differences to celebrate and which to "remediate"? How can we tell the difference between "Things I don't like or wouldn't choose" and things that are "dangerous or problematic for a child"? How will our own values and biases play into those decisions?

Do we ask the athletic, "tomboy" girl to change—to wear dresses and develop an interest in sewing rather than baseball—because she is teased? Do we require the boy who collects stamps and loves to sew to play sports and be tough? Or do we attempt to create a society that is more open and accepting of multiple ways to be in the world?

Consider the following example. We might authentically celebrate the range and variety of lunches that students bring to school as reflecting the diversity of ethnicity, religious observance, or personal preferences. But what about the child who comes to school with nothing but chips and a can of soda, or the child who has no lunch? It would seem unreasonable to celebrate those limited or nonexistent lunches as part of the "diversity of lunches children bring to school."

This is confusing terrain. One student teacher reported to me that the children in the third grade had read an article about homeless children who were living on the street. They were somewhat alarmed by what they'd read and wanted to discuss it. The teacher used this moment to say that people live in lots of different places—some in houses, some in apartment, some in trailers, and some on the streets. The list seemed hardly parallel—and did nothing to address the children's distress about poverty and homelessness. The attempt to be "positive" about differences precluded a much more serious (and important) discussion about injustice and responses to inequity and lack of resources.

There are some differences or variations that clearly seem undesirable, variations that we might agree are not consistent with human thriving. Being cold, hungry, or without shelter are not situations or conditions that people generally aspire to—or want celebrated.

The problem is that for many people, disability is seen as something "bad" to be fixed, remediated, eradicated, or altered. But what if we saw disability as human variation—to be celebrated. Is that possible?

The controversy about facial cosmetic surgery for children with Down syndrome raises some of the above questions. Some parents of children with Down syndrome have elected to have their young children undergo surgery in order to change their facial appearance, eliminating some of the telltale characteristics of the chromosomal difference. They argue that society treats people with Down syndrome poorly, and that they will increase their child's future success and broaden their possibilities by decreasing the chances that their child will be seen or "read" as having Down syndrome.

Others find the idea of subjecting children to surgery that has no purpose other than to change their appearance as completely unnecessary and very distressing. They feel that it denies that child's right to be who she is and plays into societal oppression by saying to the world—and to the child—"We'll make you look different so that people will treat you better." It is our inability to accept people who look different as worthy that forces us into a response of needing to "fix" that which is different and perceived as needing to be fixed.

Emma Van der Klift and Norm Kunc[59] trace the ways in which disability is perceived and responded to. They say that when disability is seen as "deviance," then our response is marginalization. We want the deviance out of our sight and out of our lives.

Van der Klift and Kunc argue that if we perceive disability as "deficit," then our response is one of reform: You are acceptable to us if you are like us. Many limited notions of multiculturalism look a bit like this: we welcome diversity in our midst as long as it's basically people just like us with a little bit of difference. With regard to issues of sexual orientation, for example, this often comes out as, "We don't mind that you're gay as long as you don't act on it or talk about it in any way." School responses to viewing disability as deficit often center on remediation and rehabilitation—we will get you to be like others.

A third perception of disability is as "tragedy." We feel sorry for the person with the disability, and are often patronizing or kind to them, but rarely do we see them as equals. Those to whom we give our used clothes and our money—because we feel sorry for them—are rarely the same people we invite into our homes or with whom we initiate friendships. The segregation of people with disabilities into "special" classrooms and separate lives is justified by paradigms of deficiency and deviance and tragedy. These sometimes get disguised as compassion and justified as "help." But they lead to segregation and a failure to value people for who they are.

If, however, disability were viewed as a form of diversity, if we accepted human variation as normal and valuable, then our responses would be quite different. We would reach, instead, for understanding and respect, acceptance and appreciation. These are quite different from "tolerance," which implies, "I see that you're different but I'll like you anyway," or "I'll ignore your differences in order to be friends with you." I would certainly not be happy or satisfied to have my friends say, "I tolerate being around Mara." I want my friends to see me fully—what's wonderful, what's challenging, the places I shine and the ways in which I struggle. I want their support for the places that are hard for me and celebration of the things that go well.

If we perceive disability as deviance, deficit, or tragedy, we assume that anyone who has a limitation or a disability would, ideally, *not* have that difference. It would be better, the assumption is, if deaf children could speak, if people with cerebral palsy could walk, and if hyperactive children could learn to slow down and sit still.

But if we view disability quite differently, arguing that human variation is essential to the thriving of the world and that a person's abilities and disabilities are an essential part of who they are, we don't necessarily come to this conclusion. Norm Kunc, educator, inclusion advocate, and frequent keynote speaker, is himself a person with cerebral palsy that affects both his walking and speech. He surprises audiences by telling them that if he could wake up the next day "cured" of his cerebral palsy, he wouldn't want that. Cerebral palsy is an essential part of who he is. This is a difficult concept for those who view disabilities and differences as needing to be eradicated and eliminated.

And yet there are certainly disabilities and challenges that people experience that limit their lives and their possibilities. Not being able to communicate in any way can make life very frustrating and severely alter a person's ability to control his own life. Not being able to read can deny children access to worlds of information and experience that would enrich their lives. What's the difference between abandoning people to their challenges and accepting people as they are?

At every juncture, we must continue to ask: What is my own thinking about this person's disability/difference and how does it differ from their own perception of themselves? What would be gained or lost by changing this aspect of a person's appearance, performance, location, or behavior, and how do we—and they—weigh these trade-offs? Given that there is some level of mismatch between this person's characteristics and the broader environment that is creating some difficulty—where is the "give" and on whom is change incumbent?

We return now to the idea that a good inclusion classroom is one in which we can't tell who the kids with the disabilities are. The comment sounds benign, even positive. Perhaps the visitor saw all children highly engaged or sitting and working together without physical or social marginalization. But what's the problem with the remark? Where do problems arise if we conceptualize good inclusive practices as those that mask the inclusion process itself or set as a goal that students with disabilities will pass as "normal"?

First, if the goal of good inclusion is invisibility—not being able to tell that there are kids with disabilities in the classroom—then what happens when the child in question is a child whose disability is prominent or highly noticeable? What if it's pretty obvious that Gene uses a communication device and a wheelchair with head support? What if it would be readily apparent to a visitor that a child in the class has Down syndrome or is using a braille-writing machine? Does that mean it's not a good inclusive classroom? Consider how bizarre we would find the statement, "It's a really good multicultural classroom. You can't tell that the kids are from different racial groups or speak different languages."

Second, if differences are minimized or covered up to meet a goal of making all students look the same, what messages are communicated to students about difference as opposed to variation? Isn't it better to talk about Nadia's hearing aids and what kinds of help and support she needs than to discourage the other students from noticing that she wears them, that they sometimes squeak, or that she occasionally misses important verbal cues? Is it better to accommodate Tim's diabetes and special dietary needs by inconspicuously giving him different treats at snack time so as to spare him the embarrassment of needing a special modification or to teach all the children about varying allergies, prohibitions, and requirements so they can be good allies for one another?

And third, what do we communicate to teachers and other professionals working in inclusive classrooms if we imply that good modifications and adaptations are only those that are not visible to visitors? This is not likely to encourage teachers to change what is done for or with particular children in the classroom if the goal is unnoticeable homogeneity.

Shifting our paradigm, and acknowledging the reality and value of human variation, brings us to a very different set of practices and a whole new approach to talking about diversity in a classroom community. If the goal is inclusion and the preparation of students for living in a diverse, democratic society, consider the following:

It is both positive and inevitable that differences are visible in good inclusive classrooms.

How teachers, teacher educators and other professionals respond to differences will set the tone for children, teaching them why, when and how differences should be noticed and discussed.

The goal should be to make the process of inclusion hypervisible rather than invisible, allowing all participants to engage in "inclusive thinking" and problem solving, figuring out how everyone can be included, and becoming agents for inclusive practices.

Teachers need active and ongoing support for the challenges of inclusion rather than reassurance that "good inclusion" doesn't involve changing anything or making their classrooms "look" any different.

Finally, let us return to language. Vigilance around our language must be coupled with the development of a new vocabulary for discussing human variation.

One of the most powerful shifts within the disability area has been the advocacy for what is called "people-first language." In order to make evident that we are discussing people rather than disabilities, the call is to talk about "the boy with cerebral palsy" or "the woman with the hearing impairment," rather than "the CP boy" or "the deaf woman." The goal of people-first language is to acknowledge the multiple identities people have—for example, the boy with cerebral palsy is also an African American, a Baptist, an Alabaman, and a stamp collector. He cannot be "summed up" with one label, particularly one that puts the disability first. This effort stands in strong contrast to those who refer to people with disabilities as "the wheelchairs," or "the retarded," as though an entire group of people could be referred to by their use of an assistive device or by a globalizing label used to describe a wide range of behaviors and skills.

But even this change is not unproblematic. Jim Sinclair,[60] a disability activist writes: "I am not a 'person with autism.' I am an autistic person." Sinclair says that this distinction matters to him because his autism cannot be separated from him as a person—he may wear a blue shirt one day, and a yellow shirt the next, but his autism is always part of him. He argues that saying "person with autism" suggests that the autism isn't an important part of the person, but is just one characteristic; and, for him, "autism" is central to how he sees himself, an "essential feature" of himself as a person. Further, he says that saying "person with autism" implies that autism is negative, because we don't use that terminology when describing characteristics we perceive as "positive." For example, we don't say that someone is a "person with athletic ability" but rather that he is an "athlete" or an "athletic person."

This discussion—and debate—is reminiscent of the struggles about what language is appropriate in talking about people with dark skin. A long history of oppression, political change, and personal preference have alerted us to the fact that one person's acceptable descriptor is another person's racial slur or inaccurate label. When the National Association for the Advancement of Colored People was established, the term "colored people" was considered not only acceptable, but an improvement over the common terminology of the time. Today, some people find the common term "person of color" inappropriately homogenizing, masking critical differences between people who define themselves as "Jamaican," "Haitian," "African American," "Puerto Rican," and so on.

Because of our individual histories with particular labels, people may react very differently to the same expression. I had a student object strongly to being referred to as "a Jew" and insist that she be called "a Jewish person." Even though I myself am Jewish, I did not hear the word "Jew" in the same way that she did when the speaker referred to the "contributions of the Jews to the United States." Many older people who identify as "gay" or "lesbian" are similarly uncomfortable with the use of the word "queer" as a descriptor of those who are homosexual, because to them, that word was exclusively an epithet. Others, however, have embraced the word "queer" both as a way to reclaim what had been used as a put-down and as a way of honoring the diversity of sexual identities and enactments that they feel are inadequately limited by calling people "gay" or "lesbian."

It is not uncommon to watch people outside any minority or labeled group throw up their hands in frustration, proclaiming, "How can I get it right—they keep changing the words and I'm never going to say it perfectly!" The best practice, it would seem, in all cases, is to recognize the right of each person to name herself and to recognize that people whom you may perceive as similar may, indeed, make different choices about how they want to be described.

Our process must be one of connection, relationship, and

communication; people will generally tell you—either explicitly or more implicitly—what they call themselves and what descriptors they welcome as acceptable and accurate for who they are. We must accept the fact that there is probably no one right answer, and that respect and responsiveness are always appropriate.

By the same token, it can be amusing when people bend over backward to avoid describing people using very visible and obvious characteristics. My friend Frank Hernandez, who is blind, often jokes about how embarrassed people get when they inadvertently use the word "see" in front of him, apologizing profusely, and, even in their fumbling, are unable to say the word "blind," a word he himself uses freely and comfortably.

In Buddhism and elsewhere, there are principles of "right speech" that propose that we examine every statement we make in terms of three questions. If we can't answer "yes" to all three, then we are advised not to say it! The three questions are:

1. Is it true?

2. Is it kind?

3. Is it useful?

It would not be inappropriate to ask those same three questions about how we talk about human variation. Because there is so much confusion and uncertainty about what we know to be "true" about people with disabilities, the first challenge of truth should make us hesitant to issue pronouncement such as "Retarded children can never learn to read" or

"Someone who's blind can't play on a sports team." Evidence of and appreciation for human variation should make us very reluctant to declaim with certainty about people's possibilities and futures.

The second question above—Is it kind?—is more subjective, but, in a way, also easier. I always ask myself, "Would I want someone to say this about me? About a child of mine? About someone I love?" Asking those questions would no doubt eliminate many of the things we say about people whom we perceive as different.

And, finally, asking "Is it useful?" would require us to think about whether the description or the language we are using about the person is directly related to our ability to know them well or educate them successfully. If knowing that Michael can't see the chalkboard is critical to altering his seating and providing large-print books, then certainly it makes sense to discuss his visual impairment. But if introducing someone's label or diagnosis is not directly connected to our capacity to educate, then we should rethink our language.

Acknowledging that we *all* differ in a myriad of ways should take us a giant step closer to embracing variation as "normal"—even something to be celebrated—and eliminating some fears and judgments about "the other." Similarly, by paying closer attention to our similarities and not just our differences, we are also more likely to identify shared goals and expectations for our lives and our relationships and our society. Doing this important work on language is critical to changing classrooms and teaching, which is our next focus.

7. Teaching for All and to All

Once we have an inclusive class of children—who vary and are welcomed in a million ways—then what? How is actual teaching and learning affected and changed by inclusion? I said earlier that inclusive teaching puts real demands on the classroom. That's true no matter what the subject matter. Teaching inclusively demands changes in teaching strategies and classroom structures.[61]

Luckily, this is territory where educational innovators have led the way. Many structures and ways of framing instruction have been developed and refined over the years that make schooling more accessible to a broader range of students. These include different ways for students to acquire information, to interact with new content, and to show what they have learned. As we'll see, the structures include multilevel and multigrade classrooms, differentiated instruction, peer teaching and coteaching, all methods of teaching that start from an assumption that the classroom will support a wide, diverse community of learners. None of these is sufficient in isolation, but when a curriculum is structured and supported using these practices, education improves for all students. (Later, I'll take up the question of how we continue to promote this kind of deepening and enrichment in an era in which standardized curriculum, direct instruction, and high-stakes tests threaten to limit, if not destroy, much of what we value about diversity and schooling.)

Many of these strategies require not just new forms of classroom instruction and organization, but also rely heavily on the creation of a supportive classroom learning environment. If students don't understand why their classmates are doing different things or are being required to meet alternative goals, individualization and differentiated instruction become very challenging. The more differentiation there is in a classroom, the less stigmatizing any particular modification is.

Teachers with heterogeneous classrooms who attempt to individualize instruction to meet children's needs will often be asked at first, "How come Noah doesn't do the same math we do?" or "When will I get to work on the computer like Ping does?" How a teacher responds to such questions will do much to set the tone of the classroom. Generally speaking, honest, forthright answers seem best. "Noah works in a different book because he's working on addition, and he's not ready for multiplication yet" or "Let's find a time when you can work with Ping on the computer." Most who teach in inclusive classrooms report that, after a short period of time, children accept the fact that other children may be working on different levels or materials, and they often assist other students when they can. When both needing and giving help are treated as common, natural occurrences, then children can be accommodating of one another's challenges and appreciative of their accomplishments.

When teachers are discussing student differences—who is good at what, who has trouble, and so forth—they must also talk about the fact that all students are in school to learn, all people have things they do well and things they do less well, and everyone does better with encouragement and support.

Some teachers mistakenly assume that if they do not talk about the ways in which children in their classes differ—do not comment on the fact that one child reads more slowly, that another talks with difficulty, or that still another finishes math problems before anyone else—they will somehow avoid the comparisons and competitive evaluations in which children often engage. In truth, the opposite is more likely. When teachers do not directly address differences in skills and abilities, students receive the message that certain things simply cannot be talked about, and their discomfort is likely to increase. How should teachers handle differences in academic skills and performance in their classrooms?

As has been stated earlier, eliminating star charts and other forms of competition in the classroom (spelling bees, awards for the best team, and voting on the best essay) is critical. As we saw, such competition damages students all along the academic spectrum.

Avoiding negative comparisons, however, is only the first step, and it is far from enough. Teachers must find multiple opportunities to talk about and honor children's differences and actively help them figure out ways to include their peers.

When children see that individual differences are supported in a noncompetitive classroom environment, they are free to celebrate the successes of their classmates without comparison. In one classroom I entered, a student commented to me, "Craig just got a new reading book, and he can read real stories now!" Although the child who shared Craig's accomplishment with me had been reading for many years, he was able to recognize and appreciate Craig's important milestone. Confident in his own success and supported for his own accomplishments, he understood that every child in the room was working on what he or she needed in order to learn. This is evidence, to me, of a teacher who has done an admirable job of helping students understand each others' challenges so that they can celebrate one another's triumphs.

Students are not the only ones, however, who may need support in understanding instruction that looks different—

and that doesn't include some of the typical grouping and sorting they are used to. Parents may also need to see how their child's needs can be better met by multilevel, differentiated instruction than by a segregated special education program or a pull-out gifted program.

As we have discussed before, many of us are used to segregation (even if we're not fully comfortable with it). We grew up with tracked classes, perhaps with the "special education class" in the basement, and the existence of highly selective gifted programs. We *knew* which reading group we were in, that the Bluebirds was a "higher" group than the Robins, and that the Stanford Reading Achievement color-coding system told you how competent you were as a reader. It can be challenging to conceptualize how it might work to have students of very different abilities in the same classroom, with all of their educational needs met.

Indeed, this is not an easy task. It involves rethinking many of our embedded assumptions about what it means to teach. Is it "teaching" if one has organized tightly structured learning centers through which students rotate? Is it still "teaching" if students are pursuing individual contracts that culminate in community-wide sharing?

Parents of students with disabilities may worry that their child will be teased in the regular classroom or that their educational needs won't be met. These are valid concerns that must be addressed systematically, and not through glib reassurance. Once they see, however, that their son with a cognitive disability has many more opportunities to be actively engaged in conversational interactions, for example, they may be more supportive of regular education placement. Most parents of children with disabilities want their children to grow up as part of the community in which they live, and this means going to school and interacting with chronological peers.

Perhaps more significant, many parents of "typical" children have also come to support integration or full inclusion within schools. This is particularly true as they see their children becoming comfortable with, and knowledgeable about, disabilities and differences. Even parents who initially expressed concern that the presence of children with educational challenges would "dilute" their own child's education have noted that, when conscientiously implemented, inclusive regular classrooms do not lose any of their "rigor"; rather, they become more flexible, accommodating learning environments for all children.

Parents whose children have been labeled "gifted" are often conflicted. Though they certainly want their child's educational and intellectual needs to be met and their child to feel accepted and valued, their choices may be constrained. Some parents feel that their child's unique needs cannot be met in the typical workbook-oriented, lockstepping classroom and that removal to a special class is the only solution. They are concerned that their high-achieving child will be bored or held back by less intelligent classmates. Other parents, however, worry about separating their child from his regular classmates; they do not want their child to feel stigmatized or overly different from other children. Many of these concerns, however, are a function of the inadequacy of most regular classrooms rather than inherent flaws in the principles of multilevel, multimodality classrooms. If and when parents can be shown integrated classrooms that meet the individual needs of their child within an inclusive, accepting classroom community, the potential for parental support of heterogeneous grouping will be enhanced.

What follows are possible strategies and useful concepts for engaging students in more inclusive ways while recognizing that these ways of teaching may require differences in teacher education and professional support.

COOPERATIVE LEARNING

Cooperative learning is one of the optimal ways to teach children with different abilities in the same classroom. Cooperative learning involves a heterogeneous group of students working together on a common task or project. Much of the early work in cooperative learning referred to the importance of heterogeneous grouping as one of the organizing principles, but we have more recently needed to expand the concept of heterogeneity to address strategies for including all children, including those previously segregated in special classes or programs.

It is also important to think about heterogeneity broadly, including children who differ in terms of race, ethnicity, language, family background, and skills. Teachers can make thoughtful choices for cooperative learning activities, and the student groups formed for a particular project need not be the same throughout the day. Activities should be designed to take advantage of many different kinds of skills and abilities so that the same students are not necessarily always the most skilled or proficient. Shaking things up in this way disrupts students' ideas (and our own) of who is "smart" and "valuable" by challenging the sense that there is only one continuum of "smartness" in the classroom.

Teachers must be careful not to fall into simple-minded and narrow enactments of the concept of heterogeneity, for example, saying, "I always put one high-ability student, two middle-ability students, and one low-ability student in each group." The work of Elizabeth Cohen[62] has stressed the importance of not only honoring multiple kinds of intelligence, but also structuring complex cooperative tasks that showcase different strengths and allow students to see one another as smart in different ways. If the implementation of the idea of heterogeneity simply reinforces students' perceived status in the classroom ("We have to have Wendell in our group, and he's dumb."), then cooperative learning will not improve students' learning and mutual understanding as we desire.

Living in community as adults means recognizing this same idea—that there are so many ways to be smart and that we *need* each other! Last week, when my car started making a horrible clanking noise on the highway, I was exquisitely aware that I wanted help from someone who had skills very different from mine—I could write a story about what happened on the expressway, but I wanted to interact with someone who knew how to diagnose and *fix* the noise!

In my ideal classroom, an outside visitor who asked, "Who is the smartest kid in here?" would be met by a blank stare and the question, "Smart at what?"

One cooperative method, called Jigsaw (developed by Elliot Aronson)[63] involves dividing the material to be learned into five or six parts and assigning students to heterogeneous five- or six-member teams. Each student is responsible for learning a portion of the material in an "expert" group and then teaching her portion to the whole team. Members of different groups who have been assigned the same portion of material meet in "expert groups" to study and discuss their section. Because each group member is responsible for all the material, all students must help each other learn; no one can sit back without participating.

The Jigsaw method can be used to teach many things: One second-grade teacher assigns groups of five and gives each group member two of the week's ten spelling words to teach to the rest of the group. A fifth-grade teacher required group members to learn and then teach different parts of a unit on South Africa. Group members specialized in the music, art, food, geography, or history of the region. Paula Boilard, a band teacher, divided her jazz band into groups who became "experts" in the rhythm, dynamics, articulation, and melody of a new piece.

Perhaps the most common way of organizing the classroom for cooperative learning is a model sometimes called "Learning Together"[64] (developed by David and Roger Johnson). The teacher assigns heterogeneous groups of students to produce a single product as a group. The teacher arranges the classroom to promote peer interaction, provides appropriate materials, constructs and explains the task so that it requires group cooperation, observes the students' interactions, and intervenes as necessary. Students may be placed with a partner, for example, and asked to do a complex math problem. Each member must be able to explain the answer; one cannot just say, "Because Juan Manuel said the answer is 34." Therefore, higher-achievement students must work with and teach lower-achieving students. Larger groups of four or five may be asked to produce a skit, with different group members assigned to the writing, directing, and acting.

With this method, considerable emphasis is placed on teaching group members appropriate social skills to assure smooth interaction and cooperation. One way of doing this is by assigning special tasks to each group member. If the group's objective, for example, is to generate a list of ways the school could recycle waste products, one group member might be assigned the role of recorder (writing down what people say), one the role of encourager (making sure that everyone contributes), one the role of clarifier (making sure that everyone agrees with and understands what has been written), and one the role of reporter (letting the large group know what has been recorded). These roles might be clearly described for the students on different cards, and the teacher could engage students in lessons on how to do each task: "What are some ways you could encourage other people in your group?" or "What are some clarifying questions you could ask your group members?" This explicit teaching of social skills is critical to all students in inclusive classrooms, not just to those with disability labels.

When cooperative learning is implemented in inclusive classrooms, the curriculum must be rich enough—and the task organized—so that every child has a meaningful role: A cooperative learning math group is doing complex three-step story problems. One of the group members is Jamal, whose math goals include reading and writing numerals 1 through 10. He is given the role of recorder for the group. He must write the answer on the answer sheet as it is dictated by his group members. He is also asked to read the answer back to the group to check for accuracy. In this way, he is working on his math goals within a supportive group context.

Unfortunately, for many teachers, cooperative learning has been reduced to something they do with (sometimes to) students for a brief period of the day or week. Formulaic, regimented systems of cooperative learning take away the impetus to make all aspects of the classroom and students' experience cooperative. We need to examine every part of the classroom: what we teach, how we teach it, how we organize and manage students, how we respond to questions, how we solve problems, and how we talk about concerns. Cooperative learning has the potential to be truly transformative if we use it not just to "get the job done," but also to teach students to embody a philosophy of mutual care and interpersonal responsibility.

MULTILEVEL TEACHING

Instead of assuming that all students will be engaged in identical learning experiences for the same unit and evaluated according to the same criteria, the curriculum can be conceptualized as broad and inclusive. If the class is doing a unit on space, for example, the teacher can organize space activities and projects on many different levels. Children who have exceptional reading and research skills might be asked to write a report on the origins of the galaxy. Other children might be asked to draw and label the major planets in the solar system. A child with limited language skills might be required to arrange and identify pictures of the sun, the moon, and the earth. Each student would present her completed projects to the whole group, so that everyone benefits from the diversity of activities.

In one classroom that included students identified as "gifted" and students labeled as "cognitively delayed," the teacher set up a school sandwich store. The students took teachers' orders for Friday's lunch and delivered their sandwiches on that day. All class members were involved in the project, but at different levels. Depending on their math skills, some children calculated prices according to ingredient costs, some figured out state and classroom tax, and others did the actual shopping. Students whose educational objectives included functional skills, such as meal preparation, worked to make the sandwiches. Other students generated publicity and issued a monthly business report. By constructing a project like this, the teacher was able to engage all students in a collaborative project and still meet each individual's educational needs.

Teachers continually need to challenge the traditional curriculum and ask themselves: What does each child need to know? What aspects of this unit can be modified or adapted? Can students participate in the same activity with different levels of evaluation and involvement, or does an alternative, related activity need to be provided?

By asking these questions, teachers may find that they can achieve more flexibility for the whole class, and that modifications made with a particular student in mind can benefit many students. Patty Feld implements multilevel instruction by teaching across modalities. By including reading, writing, drawing, and movement in her lessons, she is able to address the age and skill differences among her students. A unit on dinosaurs, for example, included students writing a play based on research, students creating three-dimensional dioramas, an animal pantomime activity, and the creation of a dinosaur fact rap song. Classroom posters read, "We encourage our friends"; Patty tells students that questions are always okay. She not only encourages questions but turns those questions back to the group. She says she has learned to ask open-ended questions that do not have right or wrong answers, and to wait for multiple replies. Often, a child who has not immediately jumped into the discussion later makes a contribution that enriches the conversation.

Another teacher assigned one student each day to take notes to share with the class (a copy of the student's personal notes) to meet the needs of a deaf student who could not take notes. The teacher later found that these notes were also helpful to students with learning problems who could not both listen and take notes, students whose handwriting left them with very inadequate notes, and students who were absent and needed to catch up. Another teacher, on the advice of the learning-disabilities teacher, wrote key vocabulary words on the board and taught these to the class before beginning a new lesson. She found that all students benefited from this pre-teaching motivation and organization. Another teacher, in helping one student get himself organized by teaching him to use an assignment notebook and to check with peers for assignments, found that many students in her class could benefit from a similar system to keep themselves on task and on track. Such classroom modifications and adaptations benefit children's learning and also demonstrate that all students are valued. We do not abandon people who are having difficulties.

By the same token, many activities designed for students labeled as "gifted" turn out to be simply wonderful educational experiences for all students. I was asked some years ago to work with a group of teachers who wanted to develop better curricular options for the students in their gifted programs. Midway through our week's work together, the project was completely transformed when teachers realized that if they broadened their curriculum they could meet the needs of all the students in their class. They developed what they called the "Curriculum Box Project," each teacher taking responsibility for collecting and developing a wide range of instructional and curricular options across a range of academic levels, learning modalities, and interests.

Rather than limiting the school play or the science fair only to high-achieving students, teachers have found ways to transform exciting activities so that they include everyone. Modeling after Judy Chicago's Dinner Party project, which involved creating place settings for famous women, a third-grade teacher created a similar project for all the students in her inclusive classroom. Each student chose a famous woman, found out information about her, and made a placemat that represented her. The student then role-played that woman on an evening when parents and other invited guests walked around and talked with all the "famous women." This way of organizing instruction made the project—and the learning—accessible to the children, who demonstrated a wide range of reading, writing, and speaking abilities.

MULTIPLE INTELLIGENCES

The theory of multiple intelligences was developed by Howard Gardner[65] of Harvard University in 1983. Gardner argued that the traditional notion of intelligence—as one clear continuum that could be measured by standardized IQ tests—was too narrow. Instead, he suggested that there were eight different intelligences that could be used to describe the many ways in which children and adults navigated through the world.

These have been identified as:

1. Linguistic intelligence ("word smart")

2. Logical-mathematical intelligence ("number/reasoning smart")

3. Spatial intelligence ("picture smart")

4. Bodily-kinesthetic intelligence ("body smart")

5. Musical intelligence ("music smart")

6. Interpersonal intelligence ("people smart")

7. Intrapersonal intelligence ("self-smart")

8. Naturalistic intelligence ("nature smart")

Since then, spiritual intelligence has also been added to the list by other educators.

Because schools traditionally focus most of their attention (and admiration) on people with linguistic and logical-mathematical intelligence, we often miss the other forms of intelligence and fail to cultivate or value them. Children who shine in areas that might lead them to be dancers, artists, therapists, naturalists, and designers are rarely helped to recognize their own gifts or given the tools to understand how their gifts could be valued in the broader community.

Instead, many children who excel in these areas are often undervalued, and sometimes they are actually given disability labels such as "learning disabled," "attention deficit disorder," or "underachiever."

Thomas Armstrong has been one of the major translators of the theory of multiple intelligences into educational practices that can be used to reach and teach a wide variety of learners.[66] Armstrong believes that schools (and education) would be radically transformed if teachers were trained to present their lessons in a wide variety of ways, particularly ways that actively tap into the multiple intelligences. Many of the teaching strategies already identified in this chapter are examples of teaching through multiple intelligences. The student, for example, who explains a complex task to others in a cooperative learning group is probably developing her interpersonal skills as well as the academic skills called for by the task. The student who is permitted to use his accelerated reading and writing skills to write a musical play is using many additional intelligences, including bodily-kinesthetic (stage movements and choreography), spatial skills (set design), and musical intelligence (writing music or songs).

If a teacher is having trouble teaching a particular student through more linguistic approaches, the theory of multiple intelligences provides alternative ways that students can acquire knowledge—and demonstrate what they have learned. A study of the Civil Rights movement, for example, might include studying the songs of the time or writing a song, developing role plays about key moments in the desegregation struggle, constructing a time line of events that link the Civil Rights movement with the women's movement, drawing a cartoon strip that tells the story of a particular event in the movement, interviewing community members about their memories and perceptions of the '60s, and developing a contemporary ad campaign that addresses continuing issues of racism and discrimination.

The good news about conceptualizing curriculum and teaching this way is that all students can be actively engaged in meaningful learning in ways that contribute to the overall learning of the class. Segregation into ability groups becomes unnecessary, and oftentimes, expectations of who can benefit from which project or kind of instruction are challenged. It may turn out, for example, that the child with a cognitive disability is great at participating in role-plays that reinforce her knowledge of the content being studied. Or perhaps a struggling reader discovers that reading from a script—as part of a cast of readers—greatly enhances his understanding of what he is reading and what it means to coordinate his reading contributions with others—understanding that reading has communicative function.

Virtually any content can be analyzed and taught through a wide variety of "intelligences," but this does not mean that individual students should be limited to learning or demonstrating their achievement in only one area. We must be careful, in other words, to avoid de facto tracking and segregation through a new theory. If Marcus is always asked to draw what he has learned, he may never develop his writing skills. If Carmelita always writes songs, she may not learn to draw or to express herself visually.

Understanding and implementing instruction based on the concept of multiple intelligences involves both honoring students' strengths and pushing them to improve in areas in which they don't shine and may not voluntarily choose. One teacher I know designs a broad range of curricular options and then makes individual contracts with students: The student can choose two of the activities to do, and the teacher chooses two more. Or perhaps the alternative activities are organized in the form of a menu, linking together projects or learning possibilities into different areas and then asking students to choose one from column A, one from column B, and one from column C, thereby ensuring that all students are improving in all areas, even while they have some individual choice.

DIFFERENTIATED INSTRUCTION

Differentiated instruction refers to a way of organizing teaching so that the content, activities, and products are developed to respond to varying learner needs. All students are engaged in challenging work, but there is more flexibility in terms of how specific tasks are accomplished. Students might, for example, work at learning centers, each of these focusing on a specific skill or task. Or students and teachers might develop individual contracts with students that specify what each child needs to do to meet the academic goals set for her.

Teachers using differentiated instruction often use flexible grouping, including learning in pairs, triads, quads, in student-selected groups, teacher-selected groups, random groups, and as a whole class. Rather than having students permanently pigeonholed into a particular learning group (often a group organized to be homogeneous around a particular skill or lack thereof), flexible grouping means organizing instruction so that students move through a variety of different groups every day. Sarah and Tanner might both be in a very short-term group working on the use of apostrophes, part of different cooperative learning groups that are working on a volcano project, paired with different students as reading buddies during quiet reading, and involved as peer tutors with younger children during part of math time.

As opposed to more traditional forms of teaching in which all students are asked to complete an identical assignment (a five-page book report, for example) which is then judged according to a strict rubric, the requirements in a multilevel, differentiated classroom might be to read a book (and these would vary tremendously in length and complexity) and then demonstrate what you learned from the book through a written report, a song, a drawing, an interview, a graphic organizer, a poster, or the construction of a story time line. All student projects can be shared with the whole class, allowing the student whose writing skills are less sophisticated than some to nonetheless be in a position of "expert" or teacher to the rest of his classmates.

One of the leading proponents of differentiated instruction, Carol Tomlinson,[67] says: "Our similarities make us human. Our differences make us individuals." This philosophical value becomes manifest when all students' work is valued but differs in how it is tailored to individual students' needs, strengths, and abilities. Within this context, success is viewed as "individual growth," or collective achievement, not as a competitive comparison between individuals.

UNIVERSAL DESIGN

Universal design was originally an architecture term that refers to designing buildings and physical structures so that everyone can use them. For example, rather than building stairs for people who can climb steps and building a separate entrance for those who can't, a builder might build a ramp that all people can use.

With reference to curriculum, the principle of universal design can be contrasted with the idea of retrofitting the curriculum after the fact. Rather than designing the lesson and then saying, "Uh, oh, this isn't going to work for Holly because she can't read, or for Wei because he doesn't speak much English—what shall we do for them instead?" we design the lesson *from the beginning* so that a wide range of learners can access it.

At a practical level and an ideological level, universal design is very different from planning the curriculum and *then* considering the students with divergent educational needs, because it implies that all students belong in the classroom and that the curriculum is designed for all of them. By providing broad, diverse options from the beginning, as part of the original design, teachers are much less apt to be surprised or distressed by the variation in their classrooms.

PEER TEACHING

Another way to address different skill levels within a class is to arrange for children to be resources for one another through peer tutoring or peer teaching. Such programs can be arranged at many different levels, both within classrooms and across grade levels. In one school, every sixth grader has a first-grade math "buddy" with whom he or she works three times a week. This system provides extensive one-on-one instruction for the first graders, and the sixth-grade teacher has reported that even the weakest math students in her class are showing a new interest and enthusiasm for mathematics. She has seen some of the sixth graders doing extra work to prepare for their teaching, so they would "be sure to get it right."

For peer teaching or peer tutoring to positively affect some of the typical status hierarchies within classrooms, teachers must be careful that all children get a chance to be the teacher or the leader and that no one is stuck permanently in the role of receiving help or getting help. In inclusive classrooms where the range of skills and interests is wider than usual, it is especially important that relationships be reciprocal. Students identified as having learning challenges can be given opportunities to teach as well as learn.

COTEACHING

The days in which classrooms consisted of one teacher and a group of students are long gone. Inclusive classrooms require the collaboration of a wide range of professionals, including regular education teachers, special education teachers, physical and occupational therapists, social workers, speech therapists, teachers' aides, and other professionals. Inclusive classrooms often have multiple adults working with a group of students, each bringing her own particular skills and abilities to the teaching collaboration. One of the benefits of this collaboration is that when students learn to work with a variety of adults, there is an increased chance that at least one adult will be able to establish a significant working relationship with each student.

In some collaborative inclusive classrooms, the teaching team consists of a person prepared as a special education teacher and one prepared as a regular education teacher, each bringing his own expertise to the classroom. Ideally, these two teachers work together as a smooth team, and are not viewed as having discrete responsibilities; that is, the "special education teacher" is not limited to working with students with disabilities, and the general education teacher to working with typical students. In some highly successful classrooms, the students feel that they have two teachers, and are often unaware or unconcerned about who is certified in what.

For collaboration to be successful, teachers must learn how to communicate clearly and effectively, how to share teaching responsibilities, and how to resolve conflicts in teaching styles and approaches. Dukewits and Gowin[68] argue that for teams to work collaboratively and productively, they must do five things: establish trust; develop common beliefs and attitudes; empower team members to make decisions; learn to manage meetings effectively; and become skilled in providing feedback about team functioning. Each of these skills can be learned (and taught), and each is essential to creating successful partnerships.

There are many models of collaborative teaching, including those in which both teachers work with the whole group; those in which each teacher works with a small group of students, perhaps circulating between groups; and those in which one teacher takes the lead, and the other teacher provides added support to students who need more help.

Before any of these models can be implemented, teacher need to spend considerable time planning for instruction and developing a good working relationship. They need to discuss their philosophies of education, how they view their roles, how they define their own instructional strengths, how they want to relate to one another in front of students, how they will divide responsibilities for communicating with parents, and a whole host of practical and logistical details.

Paraprofessionals also play a critical role in inclusive classrooms. One of the most frequently documented problems with the use of paraprofessionals is that they often maintain too much proximity to the student with special needs, thereby limiting that student's interaction with others. Causton-Theoharis and Malgrem outline ways in which paraprofessionals can be used to promote peer interaction by seeking out rich social environments for the student with disabilities, highlighting similarities between the student and his peers, and redirecting conversation to the student being supported rather than responding *for* the student with disabilities.[69]

Paraprofessionals can implement instructional strategies that promote student interactions, fading themselves into the background and allowing more natural social supports to develop among students.

INCLUSIVE CURRICULUM: A CURRICULUM
THAT NAMES AND VALUES DIVERSITY

Inclusive teaching is not tied to a particular content. Any subject taught in an inclusive community can be engaged using the methods in this chapter. And yet inclusion does have some major implications for the curriculum itself. It matters who is represented in the curriculum and who is left out. Given the mission and relationships embedded in the inclusive classroom, it matters that all children feel that they are part of the curricular focus.

This can be, at one level, a matter of representation. What books are in the book corner? Are there books that represent a wide range of different families: adoptive, biracial, and extended families? Families with parents who are separated, divorced, single, gay, or lesbian?" Who's on the wall? Are there pictures of men and women of color, such as Rosa Parks, Cesar Chavez, Wilma Mankiller, Louis Rodriguez, and Audre Lorde?

What religions are celebrated or discussed in the classroom? Do students learn about Jewish, Buddhist, Muslim, Hindu, and Baha'i holidays? Are they taught how to respect classmates who are fasting or observing different rituals?

Are all adults/guardians/relatives welcomed on "Parents' Night," perhaps occasioning a new name for the open house? Does the unit on careers take into account that some students have parents who are unemployed, incarcerated, deceased, or employed in activities students are not comfortable discussing?

Whose books are read? Whose poetry is shared? What music is played? What songs are sung? What art decorates the walls? Whose languages find their way into the classroom acoustic environment?

Do field trips, book orders, holiday parties, and snack time make differences in socioeconomic levels visible and painful, or do the school and teacher make sure that all students can fully participate in all activities without stigma or "charity"?

When issues of difference are raised—whether innocently or unkindly—how do teachers respond? In one classroom, four first graders were working at the writing table. A little girl (I'll call her Frances) turned to another and said (in a somewhat provocative tone), "You're Puerto Rican!" Overhearing this comment, the teacher responded immediately and directly, "Don't say that!" Although the teacher's intention was no doubt to reprimand or challenge what sounded like a negative tone at best or a racist comment at worst, what message did the students get? Don't mention that Maria is Puerto Rican? (She was!) It's not good to talk about *being* Puerto Rican?

If not at that precise moment, perhaps soon, the discussion could quickly have shifted to an understanding of what it means to be Puerto Rican, where Puerto Rico *is*, or Maria's experiences on the mainland since she got here. We might also want to know why Frances made that comment: What was she noticing or thinking? This is as much a curricular issue as it is one of social climate—simply telling students not to call one another names isn't sufficient. We also need to educate, in this case, perhaps, about accents, bilingualism, immigrant communities, and Spanish in addition to emphasizing kindness, respectful questioning, and welcoming language.

When the climate for discussion is welcoming of all questions, then it is easier to discuss why Gloria's hearing aids sometimes squeak, or why Carlin can get out of her wheelchair sometimes but why Annyah can't. It becomes possible to brainstorm how Gregory can be included in the school chorus although he doesn't speak or how Malina can participate in playground games with support. We can even talk about more challenging situations: What should students do when Grayson starts yelling and pinching people? How can students stay safe and still support Grayson? How can they find other times and ways to engage Grayson during the school day?

Not only does the overall arrangement and climate of the classroom communicate whether or not difference is valued, but what we teach specifically can also be broadened to explicitly value diversity.

Including information about issues of diversity—and even disability—can begin with even very young children. A unit on the five senses, for example, can include information on vision and hearing impairments—what is it like to need glasses or a hearing aid? What's helpful to a person who doesn't hear well? A unit on fairy tales can include a discussion of characters that feel different, such as the Ugly Duckling or Rumpelstiltskin, and can extend into a discussion of labeling and stereotypes. Even very young children can understand issues of access and barrier-free design by going on a walking tour of their school or neighborhood and noting the impediments to full participation.

For older students, studying World War II and the Holocaust is a powerful time to discuss the different groups who were murdered by the Nazis in their quest for a "perfect society." Many students know only about the persecution of the Jews and aren't aware of the systematic persecution and murder of people with disabilities, gays and lesbians, Catholics, unionists, Gypsies, and the elderly. Studying Japanese internment camps provides an opportunity to discuss what happens when fear of the "other" becomes so extreme that we recreate (here in the United States) discrimination and persecution of U.S. citizens of Japanese descent at the same time that we are espousing justice elsewhere.

As I write this, there are ongoing protests and student and teacher walkouts related to immigration policies. Understanding the history of immigration to the United States and the ways in which various groups were or were not welcomed will help students make clear connections to issues of diversity and inclusion: How can people be "illegal"? What are students' own experiences relative to people from other countries? How many students have immigrant parents, grandparents, or great-grandparents? What can our surnames teach us about our countries of origin?

Because much of history is taught as a history of struggle and conflict between two groups, it is also important for students to learn about social movements and historical events that featured people working together cooperatively—and across diverse racial, ethnic, and linguistic lines—to reach a common goal. In their book *Cooperative Learning, Cooperative Lives,* authors Nancy Schniedewind and Ellen Davidson share lessons for teaching students about the American Red Cross, for example, or the formation of labor unions, as examples of people working together.[70]

Much of this echoes ideas of "multicultural education," and indeed such education is a natural component of inclusive classrooms. But we must move beyond what is often called the "additive approach" or the "contributions approach." Holding an ethnic foods potluck and putting "children of many lands" on the bulletin board are wonderful, but they won't substantially alter our understandings or attitudes toward diversity. We need, rather, to implement what Banks has labeled "transformative" multicultural education,[71] an approach that includes social action. Describing this approach as "education that is multicultural" as opposed to "multicultural education"[72] enforces that everything that happens in school should be embedded with a worldview of diversity, rather than inserting diversity issues as an afterthought or separate entity, as in "It's February—now let's learn some African American history." We can situate multicultural education within a far more political and activist framework, enabling student to not only view concepts, issues, and events from diverse perspectives, but linking their analysis to action related to injustice, prejudice, and discrimination.

This broader vision clearly embraces the inclusion of students with disabilities, particularly as it discusses a richly diverse society (which includes people with disabilities) and the importance of including the voices and experiences of all people.

INCLUSIVE EXTRACURRICULAR ACCESS

Just as the academic curriculum needs to be reconceptualized to include every child, so too must extracurricular activities be redefined for inclusion. If participating in sports, music, art, and other "extras" is seen as a right or privilege only for high-achieving students, or, if students with disabilities are seen as unable to participate or benefit, then full inclusion becomes highly unlikely.

Rigid ways of viewing extracurricular activities limit the participation not only of students with disabilities, but also of those who are "different" racially, linguistically, or economically. Students who must work while in high school to help pay for their supplies are unlikely to be able to be part of sports teams that travel on weekends and require elaborate uniforms. If speaking fluent English is a requirement for participation in theater and music activities, other students will also be eliminated. Attitudes of exclusion affect all of us, not just students with disabilities.

In responding to some of these barriers, Paula Kluth and I articulated a vision of what inclusive extracurricular activities could look like,[73] including the following:

• Understand that all students can learn something from participating in extracurricular activities. A student who cannot physically participate in the game of basketball can serve as a team manager, statistician, game photographer, motivational coach, or free-throw expert.

• Value participation over competition. Rather than counting the number of trophies in the class cases or the number of years the school has been invited to the mathematics decathlon, educators might congratulate themselves on how many students join and participate in school-sponsored activities, perhaps issuing an "inclusion index" for the school that documents how many hours students spend learning beyond school, or how many students tried a new activity for the first time during the year.

• Allow every student the right to participate in extracurricular activities. Withholding participation in extra-curricular activities as a form of behavioral management often backfires, removing students from the one positive aspect of schooling they experience. I know many students who would not have stayed in or finished high school had they not been heavily invested (and supported) in sports, drama, music, or the arts.

• Commit to expanding extracurricular options to include a broader range of interests and needs. In one school, students can choose from groups that include: salsa dance, ultimate Frisbee, vegetarian society, pen pal club, debate club, ham radio, and future veterinarians. A student with autism had a difficult time with all of the competitive sports offerings at his school, so his principal encouraged him to launch a comic book drawing and discussion group. Not only was it a perfect fit for the learner with autism, but it also attracted several art students and a host of comic book fans.

It is through participation in school extracurricular activities that many people learn who they are and what they enjoy, activities and identities that they build on after they leave school. The student who participates in music activities in school is more likely to join the community choir; students who enjoyed physical activities in high school are more likely to be engaged in such activities as adults.

For the last several years, I have led workshops titled Music Making for All. These sessions include songs without words, songs with sign language, songs with different parts, rounds, and songs that are done as call and response. Each type of music has characteristics that allow for full (not partial) participation by all members. It is important to remember that full participation does not mean that every person is doing the same thing at the same time. Full participation means that everyone has an active and valued role (not just holding up the applause sign at the end).

Recently, I have also been teaching Movement for All

classes, helping everyone to find joy in her body and movement, regardless of size, grace, or previous experience with dance. By structuring activities that are fun and that allow multiple levels and forms of participation, everyone has a wonderful time, gets some exercise, and interacts playfully with others. And by doing these workshops in an inclusive manner, everyone in the group (including the most graceful) gets to witness that there are many ways to be involved, even if that looks quite different from what the viewer is doing. At a recent workshop, a young man with autism spent the entire dance workshop running around the periphery of the room, sometimes stopping to engage with others, other times rocking and dancing by himself. At the end of the period, however, he used a letter board to spell out his reaction: "This was wonderful. I wish I could dance everyday. But I don't like sitting on the floor—next time, pillows." I am sure that his response surprised those in the group who had seen him as a nonparticipant or as unaware of his surroundings. For many people, reclaiming music and movement means recovering from the messages they got growing up and at school—that music is only for those who can "really sing," or that dance is only for those who are slim and graceful. Creating fully inclusive school communities benefits all students by expanding their repertoires and giving them new ways to learn and grow. It also profoundly alters how we see the "other," how we make judgments about who is a community member, and how we see our involvement in building a sense of belonging. Participation in extracurricular activities—another way of being a full member of one's school community—is an important precursor to being a vital member of the greater community and society.

TEACHING SOCIAL SKILLS

Another important aspect of the curriculum that is crucial to successful inclusion is the purposeful and conscientious focus on teaching social skills. I have rarely visited a classroom in which students were thoughtful and kind without finding a teacher who actively modeled this behavior and included many kinds of teaching (direct and indirect) about how we treat one another.

Students in inclusive classrooms need to learn elaborate repertoires regarding the concept of "help," for example. What does it mean to help someone? What's the difference between helping someone and doing it for them? What does "respectful help" look like and feel like?

We need to establish classroom norms and practices that are based on the belief that *all* people need help, that giving and getting help are *good* things (and not a sign of weakness), and that supporting one another strengthens the community. In an inclusive classroom, it is also important to disrupt hierarchies of who can help and who needs help, structuring situations and modeling that everyone can both give support in some way and benefit from assistance as well. We want to model behaviors that allow all people to safely be vulnerable (letting people see where they struggle and what they need) and powerful (proudly claiming their strengths and gifts without fear of reproach or anger).

Similarly, students may need to be taught other social skills that promote a welcoming school community. How does one encourage someone who is having a hard time? What kinds of appreciations are likely to be experienced as positive? What do you do when you disagree with someone or when someone is doing something that bothers you? What does it mean to compromise or find the middle ground? How can you ask questions when you don't understand? What should you do if you're really upset and need someone to talk to or to comfort you?

Certainly we all know adults who lack these skills, so it should come as no surprise that teachers may need to teach them explicitly to students. What a different world it would be if people freely and easily complimented others, offered assistance, acknowledged people's contributions, asked respectful questions when they didn't understand, and automatically reached for a decision that met everyone's needs!

STRUGGLING FOR INCLUSIVE CURRICULUM AND PEDAGOGY

Unfortunately, the kinds of curriculum and pedagogy detailed in this chapter—curriculum that is rich, diverse, draws on multiple narratives and histories, and explores diversity issues explicitly; and teaching strategies that allow flexibility, responsiveness, and individualization—are seriously under attack because of current government mandates such as No Child Left Behind. And because rich curriculum and pedagogy support the inclusion process, the near-exclusive reliance on standardized, high-stakes tests and rigid, scripted curricula directly challenges inclusive education.

As I said earlier, when teachers know that their students will be tested on a very narrow range of materials, they are often explicitly discouraged from broadening curricular possibilities. Many of the learning experiences that are most powerful—and most likely to involve the broadest range of students—have been virtually eliminated by current regimes of testing. The school play, the field trip to the zoo, the mock election, and the science fair have been eliminated in many schools. Not only that, but current mandates have led many schools to completely abandon instruction in science and social studies, further narrowing the curriculum. In addition, the ways in which test results are publicized and determine individual schools' viability (low scores can close a school) mean that it is not in any school's best interest to accept and attempt to educate learners whose needs require more intensive intervention. Students with learning or behavior challenges, students who will require additional social services, students who don't speak English well—all of these students have the potential to bring down school scores, jeopardizing the school's future. This hardly creates a situation in which schools or districts warmly welcome a wide range of students, eager to develop a cohesive learning community that embraces diversity as a positive feature.

We should not confuse having standards with standardized testing. It is reasonable to want to know that all students are learning and that teachers are taking adequate responsibility for their students' learning. But there are many ways to evaluate learning and hold learners and teachers accountable that do not involve letting standardized tests become the engine that drives instruction. As we will see at the end of the chapter, it is possible to create truly inclusive schools—and respond to the mandates of NCLB—without sacrificing children or curriculum standards.

In a recent book, *Many Children Left Behind: How the No Child Left Behind Act Is Damaging Our Children and Our Schools*, numerous educators document these and other damaging effects of the federal law.[74] To me, however, the greatest damage is in the area of trust. Public education demands trust at many levels: Parents must believe that the schools are acting in their children's best interests; students must trust that their teachers really want them to learn and succeed, and teachers must trust that they will be given adequate support to accomplish the Herculean tasks set before them. NCLB has challenged all of these levels of trust. Many parents are alarmed by what has happened to their children's education, not just the focus on testing and the distortion and diminution of the curriculum, but also by school closings for "low-achieving" schools, lack of support for struggling children, and the ways in which their own perceptions of those children's needs have become unwanted.

Teachers often report that they feel as though their job and their profession have changed remarkably. One teacher reported to me, practically in tears, what it was like to have to test children—over and over again—whom she knew could not answer the questions. She felt she was inflicting pain on them—reinforcing to them that they were not capable or smart—rather than being able to teach them. In one California school, outside monitors visit classrooms, and if teachers are not on the page that they should be for that day, they are subject to reproach and negative consequences. They must also not have anything on their walls that doesn't mesh with a state standard. It is hard to encourage creative, dedicated people to enter the field of teaching when they see that they will be asked to become "curriculum deliverers" with scripted lessons and very little time to respond to what *they* perceive as children's needs.

There is good news, however. It is possible to implement inclusive standards, documenting children's learning and growth, while still allowing students to participate in a general education experience. Kluth and Straut explain that to make standards inclusive, they must be developmental and flexible, use a wide range of assessment tools, and allow equitable access to meaningful content.[75] The many forms of instruction described in this chapter must be assessed creatively. If many students are involved in a learning experience, but working on different aspects of the curriculum, the assessment must be individualized so that each student is held accountable for her own learning, but without assuming that all students will be learning the same thing or can be assessed in the same way. If, for example, students are working on a map activity, most of the students may be held accountable for explaining what a "border" between two countries means, and how these are established and maintained. Another student working in the same group might be held accountable for being able to label the United States, Mexico, and Canada on a map, an objective geared to her learning needs or individualized educational goals. By tailoring the assessments, it isn't necessary to remove this student to a separate location with a different activity, but the multiple levels of activity and learning can each be described and assessed within the context of a common activity.

When George Theoharis took over as principal of Falk Elementary School in Madison, Wisconsin, half of the K–5 elementary school's five hundred students were living at the poverty level, and more than half were students of color; twelve different languages were represented in the student body. The school was identified, according to NCLB standards, as a "school in need of improvement." Faced with this situation—low-achieving school, a proliferation of programs, and a diverse student body—Theoharis could have done what many schools are doing. He could have narrowed the curriculum, concentrated students' and teachers' energy on test preparation, and tried to eliminate from the school program (and testing protocols) students who would bring down the school's scores. He chose, instead, to approach the school's challenges from an inclusive perspective.

The school had previously been almost exclusively white and middle class, and the changes in the school population had resulted in a proliferation of segregated programs. Students in special education were pulled out to self-contained classrooms, physical therapy and occupations therapy services were delivered almost exclusively as pull-out programs, as were speech, English as a Second Language and Title I services. The small number of students identified as gifted and talented were also pulled out. Theoharis described the school as a "bunch of random programs."

Theoharis worked long and hard with faculty, staff, parents, and students to build an inclusive school that met all students' individual needs within a context of *one* school community. Special education teachers were assigned to work with regular class teachers and became part of grade-level teams. Self-contained programs were eliminated, and all students were served in age-appropriate classrooms. Students who spoke English as a second language were clustered by language in typical classrooms and specialists came in, each working with small groups of students and teachers. Title I teachers became part of grade-level teams, and gifted and talented students were served by increasing teachers' skills in differentiating instruction.

These changes were accompanied by huge changes in the curriculum. According to Theoharis, through the new inclusive curriculum, "all the kids had access to the good stuff. And the good stuff was being delivered by more than one person." The literacy curriculum was redone, and a literacy coach modeled the new program and teamed with teachers. Staff development funds were used to release teachers so they could plan, and much of the curriculum money was used to build a huge trade book room that all teachers could access. A new hands-on science curriculum that allowed more students access to the content was chosen. A new math curriculum that promoted active student involvement and focused on mathematical thinking was adopted. New staff were not added, but the adults worked differently together to meet the needs of all the students.

Theoharis explains: "We have responsibility to all of our kids. We have data to show it's not a zero sum game."

Indeed, within a three-year period, the school went from having only half the students at grade level to 86 percent at grade level. The school went from having 13 percent to 60 percent of the special education students performing at grade level. Theoharis says, "We didn't have fewer kids performing at high levels—we had more kids performing at proficient/advanced. And the students who started out strong benefited from having more than one adult working with them as well."

Two years later, the school was removed from the list of schools in need of improvement. Although noteworthy, however, this is not what makes Theoharis proud. He notes that there are many high-achieving schools that are not inclusive, but his school is a hopeful example of alternative ways to meet federal mandates and still "do the right thing" for all students. He is heartened by the fact that implementing more inclusive curriculum and pedagogical practices can bring higher achievement for all.

How did this happen? It's important to understand that this happened over time and through the work of many people. But it also happened because of strong leadership and a powerful commitment to inclusion. "What mattered was that inclusion was not negotiable," Theoharis says. "We never had a vote on this. My stance was more, 'This is the direction we're going, and we're going to figure out how to get there together. These are the resources, and you can do this. We're going to support you as well as we can.'" Teachers were given the charge and the vision, but they were not abandoned with a handshake and a "good luck" speech. This was a process, and the whole school was involved.

Theoharis reports that some parents who were worried that "this kid will take away attention from my kid" shifted to acknowledging that everyone in the school, including their child, was doing better. Parents of students who *weren't* in special education saw that their children were also benefiting from working with more adults and from the wide range of curricular options. Theoharis says, "We made it work because exclusion simply wasn't a choice."

There are many challenges to inclusion: Both gifted programs which provide quality education to some while neglecting others and special education programs that segregate students unnecessarily draw energy and attention away from providing a good education for all.[76] Public schooling cannot engage in educational apartheid or triage programs that provide a good education only for some and mediocre programs for most. For our public school system—and our nation—to survive, we must genuinely meet the needs of all learners within inclusive communities of respect and support.

8. Taking a Stand for Social Justice

By this point, it should be evident that inclusion is not a special education issue. It is not about "letting" students with disabilities attend regular classes. It is not a favor for a particular group of people. It is, rather, a gift we give to ourselves, a way of seeing all people as interconnected and realizing that any solution must address every person. Inclusion is about reconceptualizing classrooms so that they meet the needs of diverse groups of learners. Inclusion is about acceptance. Inclusion is about belonging. Inclusion is about seeing all people (including ourselves) as complex and valuable.

Neither is inclusion only a school issue. Inclusion is about creating a society in which all people are valued and embraced as important members of the community. Inclusion is about creating citizens who understand that responding positively to diversity is an essential component of creating a democratic society in which all voices are heard. Inclusion is about understanding—and believing—that the only way for young people to learn about living in diverse, democratic communities—is by being part of one. We cannot simply teach about the values of inclusion and respect for diversity; it must be experienced in order to be real and to be understood as both desirable and possible.

Students who are in inclusive schools now will become adults employed in various capacities and connected through various social, political, and recreational communities. Those who have seen successful inclusion in action will understand that the decisions they make about where and how to live, work, and play have the potential to affect their own and others' quality of life. It is certainly possible to teach a social justice curriculum in a fairly homogeneous school by talking and teaching about overcoming prejudice, avoiding stereotypes, building allies, and addressing inequities. But inclusive classrooms give us the opportunity to put social justice principles into action; in inclusive classrooms, students can *live* a social justice curriculum and not just study about it.

A student who had a classmate with autism or one who used an alternative communication device will understand that the ability to talk well is not the only marker of capability or value. Students who have been friends with those who speak languages other than English will understand the gifts of becoming multilingual and will not equate intelligence with command of the English language.

The student who has learned to support a classmate with emotional and behavioral challenges will be far less likely to be frightened or reluctant to interact with other adults whose behavior is atypical. Those who have moved through their own fear in connecting with others who look, sound, or act different will take those skills with them into the world.

Exploring curriculum from many perspectives will help future citizens to ask, "Is there another way to look at this?" "Does everyone feel the same?" "What might account for differences in perceptions of feelings?" "What's the rest of the story?" They will be able to, as Cynthia Ozick says, "seek the story in the stranger."

Those who have been taught through strategies that better engage their own skills and gifts are much more likely to seek creative strategies for engaging others in the workplace and the community, asking, "Is there another way to do this?" "How can I make sure that everyone here is meaningfully engaged in the task?" They will know that there are so many ways to be smart and that each of us smart in different ways.

And perhaps most important, those who have experienced

genuine acceptance and belonging—a deep knowing that they are okay and valued in all their complexity—will be better able to reach out to others, seeking the (sometimes) hidden gifts in others and forming relationships that matter.

Inclusion is, at its heart, a matter of social justice. Being in an inclusive environment makes social justice *real*. Through the lessons we learn in inclusive classrooms—how to challenge exclusion, see things from different perspectives, and develop the courage and the strategies to respond to oppression—we can create the inclusive, democratic society that we envision for our children and ourselves.

This chapter focuses on the ways in which inclusive schooling can help students learn skills essential for becoming engaged members of a democratic society.

NOTICING INJUSTICE: IF YOU'RE NOT OUTRAGED, YOU'RE NOT PAYING ATTENTION

Young people are exquisitely attuned to issues of fairness. Who among us hasn't heard a child proclaim, "That's not fair!" when they have noticed something that strikes them as wrong. Sometimes, of course, that pronouncement is about not having gotten what they want—the red Popsicle instead of the green one, or the privilege of staying up as late as their older brother. But we should be careful not to dismiss children's outrage about unfairness without serious consideration. Sometimes, what children are noticing are fundamental societal and structural injustices that should be addressed. The outraged student today can, with support and education, become the committed, involved citizen of the future.

When I conducted a study of students' and teachers' perceptions about gifted programs,[77] many of the students *not* in the gifted program were acutely aware of what the students in the program were doing.

In the earlier grades, students often asked, "How come I don't get to be part of the Science Olympiad?" or "When will I get to go to the symphony concert like they do?" "Can I be in the play those kids are doing?"

Some teachers reported that they were deeply uncomfortable explaining these discrepancies to students, because it forced them to articulate policies and practices that they themselves often found problematic. One teacher said, "I tell them to talk to the school psychologist. I'm not going to be the one to tell them that they're not smart or didn't do well enough on a test." A principal told of how painful it was to tell a boy, new to the school, who asked when it would be his turn to go to the gifted program, that he would probably never have the opportunity to go.

How often is it our *own* discomfort with unfairness and injustice that keeps us from explaining these issues to children or sharing their shock and surprise? I remember, as a child, traveling to the South with my parents. It was 1959, and it was the first time I had ever seen *three* bathrooms to accommodate one population. One was marked "Men," one "Women," and the last "Colored." I tried to ask my parents what this was about; even as an eight-year-old, I knew this was wrong. I even recall saying, "But isn't that against the law?" I had thoroughly internalized all the rhetoric of "liberty and justice for all," and this seemed a clear violation. I assumed that when something was against the law, that meant it couldn't happen! I was very upset about what seemed deeply unfair and painful to me, but I received very little response from my parents. Now, many years later, I suspect that they were themselves very upset by what we were all witnessing, but, at the time, I wanted my outrage shared and validated. I wanted more information, and I wanted to know how they (and I) could do something about this injustice.

In a wonderful children's song, David Heitler-Klevans helps children understand the difference between a true injustice that should be corrected, and an outcome that wasn't as you had hoped but needs to be accepted.[78] It is important not to silence children's concerns about fairness and to help them make important distinctions between things they don't like and injustices that should be addressed:

That's Not Fair

My mom took my brother and me to a show
The performers asked for volunteers.
I raised my hand, but my brother got picked
I could feel my eyes fill up with tears.
I turned to my mom, and said "That's not fair!"
and my mom said what she always says:

"Life isn't always fair
and you won't always get a turn.
You're not the only one;
It's just something you'll have to learn."
At the break, we went to the concession stand
to get ourselves a drink and a snack.
A man cut right in front of us,
when he really should have been in the back.
I turned to the man and said "That's not fair!"
and he said what my mom always says:

"Life isn't always fair
and I'm not gonna wait my turn.
You're not as big as me;
It's just something you'll have to learn."

But what about the times when it's really not fair?
And what about the ones who don't get their share?
Should you really pretend that you just don't care?
When you come across the times when it's really not fair?
After the show, we were walking home
We saw a man asleep by the street.
I thought about how he had to live in the cold
while we have blankets, beds and heat.
I turned to my mom, and said "That's not fair!"
and she almost said what she always says, but she
> *stopped*
and said instead:

"I guess that there are times when it's really not fair
I guess that there are those who don't get their share.
We can't pretend that we just don't care
When we come across the times when it's really not
> *fair."*
I thought about what's fair and what is not
I tried to make it all make sense.
I'll try to change what I can and accept what I can't
And I'll learn to tell the difference.
'Cause sometimes when I say "That's not fair!"
I have to learn I can't get my way—

But there are also times when it's really not fair
And there are also those who don't get their share

We can't pretend that we just don't care
When we come across the times when it's really not fair.

I wanna play my part and do my share—
I'm gonna live my life to make the world more fair!

Being in inclusive environments can help hone students' understanding about issues of exclusion, oppression, and injustice. Teachers and parents can validate students' perceptions of unfairness—so that they can then learn to take action in realistic and age-appropriate ways.

Dana Williams talks about taking her six-year-old son to a pizza restaurant where they witnessed a teenager (with his parents' chuckling approval) mocking a young man in a wheelchair, imitating his noises and rocking motion.[79] Williams expressed her distress to the teasing teen and then used this episode as the occasion to engage her son in a discussion of the event, asking him why he thought the teenager was making fun of the boy with a disability and what he thought he should do about it. The six-year-old was able to articulate that no one wants to be made fun of, so they shouldn't make fun of others, and that, if you see someone being made fun of, you should stick up for them.

Even very young children can be engaged in discussions of fairness and justice. We can encourage children to notice rather than turn their heads and feign indifference or obliviousness. Discussing the daily news about the treatment of immigrants and people of color provides frequent examples. Noticing how boys and girls are treated differently in school or how students whose behavior is nonconforming are treated also provides many "teachable moments for social justice." Simply being in proximity to difference can certainly lead to noticing: "Why does that boy talk that way?" "How come her skin is so much lighter than mine?" "Why doesn't Isaac eat pepperoni pizza?" "Why did Margarita bring two women to parents' night?"

But to turn that noticing into compassionate knowing, we must have relationships with a wide range of people who are *not* like us—whom we, or others, perceive as different. Becoming friends with a classmate whose speech is challenging and learning to understand what he is saying leads us to ask different questions, not just ones of curiosity: How can I learn to communicate better? Why do people think that people whose speech is different aren't as smart? Noticing skin color as an abstract difference is one thing, but having friends with varying skin colors helps us to see and understand prejudice and discrimination, and so it too leads us to different questions. Until I became close friends with a woman of color, I was often oblivious to the subtle and not so subtle ways in which she was treated as a black woman. Until we were in a close enough relationship to trust one another with our stories, I didn't hear what happened to her in a local supermarket where she was followed or what people assumed about her based on her skin color. Inclusion helps us to develop relationships with others so that we can hear others' stories, notice justice and injustice, and have a vested interest in how our classmates and our fellow citizens are treated.

THE COURAGE TO TAKE A STAND

But noticing is not enough; as the fourteenth Dalai Lama said, "It is not enough to be compassionate—you must act." Acting can take courage; taking a stand for social justice implies risks to one's own position and status. The lyrics of the song "Courage" by Bob Blue, which are reproduced in the second chapter, is evidence of this. The young girl, noticing the exclusion of her classmate Diane, says, "I couldn't be friends with Diane, or soon they would treat me like her." By the end of the song, however, she has resolved to take a stand—in this case, by inviting Diane to the party from which she has been excluded.

Individual acts of courage may seem small, but there is no single act that doesn't matter. Gandhi said, "Whatever you do may seen insignificant, but it is most important that you do it." Even young children can learn that working for social justice can start small.

It can be tempting to believe that by staying silent, not making a fuss, not calling attention to injustice—or to ourselves—that the problem will go away and that we (personally) will be safe. But, unfortunately, this is rarely the case. As poet, feminist, and nonfiction writer Audre Lorde said, "Your silence will not protect you."

The famous poem by Pastor Martin Niemoller, written after the Holocaust, says:

First they came for the Communists,
and I did not speak out because I was not a
Communist.
Then they came for the trade unionists,
and I did not speak out because I was not a trade
unionist.
Then they came for the Jews,
and I did not speak out because I was not a Jew.
Then they came for me,
and there was no one left to speak out for me.

In contrast, a song called "Stand Up,"[80] written by Mike Stern with additional lyrics by Charlie King and Karen Brandow, presents a different vision of a similar situation:

First they came for the Communists
Then they came for the Jews
But I wasn't a Communist
And I wasn't a Jew
So I didn't stand up
And I didn't ask why
By the time they came for me
There was no one left to even try.
Then they came for the pacifists
And they came for the priests
But I wasn't a pacifist
And I wasn't a priest
So I didn't stand up
And I didn't ask why
By the time they came for me
There was no one left to even try.
Then they came for the unionists
And they came for the gays
But I wasn't a unionist
And I wasn't gay
So I didn't stand up
And I didn't ask why
By the time they came for me
There was no one left to even try.
Now they come for Muslims
And they come for the refugees
Though I am not a Muslim
And I'm not a refugee

Now I will stand up
And I will ask why
And when someday they come for me
I hope there's someone standing by my side.
Yes, we will stand up
Yes, we will ask why
And if someday they come for you
There'll be lots of people standing by your side
A world of people standing side by side.

We must all learn—and teach—that there is no such position as "neutral." To remain neutral in the face of injustice is to take a stand.

In a recently produced DVD titled "... and Nobody Said Anything: Uncomfortable Conversations about Diversity,"[81] a young college student tells her story. Although born in Pennsylvania, she identifies as Palestinian, since both her parents are from Jordan, and she makes frequent trips to the Middle East to visit her extended family. On September 12, 2001 (the day after the attacks on the World Trade Center), she went to class, and the teacher encouraged all students to speak their thoughts and feelings about what had happened. One young man, whom this student describes as one of her closest friends at the time, announced that he thought that "all Palestinians should be killed—so they can't do this to other people." The young Palestinian American, shocked, horrified, and envisioning all her young Palestinian cousins, began to cry.

Neither the other students nor the teacher said anything. The silence was profound and profoundly disturbing.

The verbal attacks on Palestinians in general and indirectly on the young woman and her family continued unchecked for fifteen minutes. This is an example of powerful silences, silences that leave scars on all those who waited, often in vain, for *someone* to say *something*. This powerful lesson is repeated over and over again in schools, usually in less dramatic circumstances; students witness verbal abuse and exclusion daily whenever they hear the words "retard," "faggot," "fatso," and other epithets used. How can we help them understand that letting things go rarely fixes things and often leads to escalation and more dangerous behavior?

LEARNING TO TAKE A STAND: STRATEGIES FOR CHALLENGING INJUSTICE

Two important quotes can guide our understanding of this last, and most important step:

> "Never doubt that a small group of thoughtful, committed citizens can change the world. Indeed, it's the only thing that ever has." —Margaret Mead

> "Let us not become the evil that we deplore."
> —Barbara Lee

Once students are aware of and knowledgeable about the injustices (big and small) that they observe, they can become engaged in "doing something." Like the seventh graders who wrote letters about inaccessible classrooms and movie theaters, other students can come to see themselves as able to make a difference, to change things:

Students in Barbara Skolnick Rothenberg's first grade at Fort River Elementary School wrote letters to the local newspaper, the governor, and their state representatives asking that the Massachusetts Turnpike signs *not* picture a Pilgrim's hat with an arrow through it! They explained how unfair it was to imply that the Native Americans attacked the Pilgrims. The turnpike sign was changed, and first graders got real proof that they could make a difference.

When pizza was ordered for the second-grade class party, the children, knowing that Joshua was a vegetarian, that Rachel kept Kosher, and that three other students were Muslim and didn't eat pork, thought about what they should order so that *everyone* would have something to eat.

In Jose Cadillo's sixth-grade class at Fort River Elementary School in Amherst, Massachusetts, a teachable moment arose when the students discussed how the post office decides whom to honor with commemorative stamps. The students conducted research on the race and gender of recent "honorees" and discussed prominent absences. They discussed who *they* thought should be honored. They began a letter-writing campaign urging the U.S. Postal Service to issue a commemorative stamp to honor James Armistead Lafayette, a former slave who served the Marquis de Lafayette and General George Washington as an espionage agent during the siege of Yorktown in 1781.

When students in the fourth grade saw how badly some girls felt about the "Daddy-Daughter Dance" because they didn't have fathers or their fathers couldn't attend—and sometimes couldn't afford the costs—they voted to change the name and concept of the event so that all students could participate, regardless of their family configuration or economic situation.

Students can be helped to notice omissions. Who isn't represented in the textbook, on the student council, in our city government? Are we ever going to read any books by women? Can we learn a song in a language *other* than English?

They can be encouraged to ask about every situation and practice—including who gets on the honor roll, how teams are chosen, how reading groups are formed, how children talk to one another—does this build community or does it damage it? Does doing things *this* way bring us closer together or push us farther apart?

Perhaps one of the simplest and most profound things that children can do is to learn to be active allies to those who are being teased or harassed in some way. Many students experience or hear teasing on a daily basis. Developing response strategies can move students from victims and bystanders to powerful change agents.

The children's book *Say Something* (by Peggy Moss) is described in chapter 2 of this book. In *Say Something,* a young girl moves from feeling proud and self-congratulatory because she doesn't *participate* in teasing and excluding others to an understanding that her silence is collusion—that she must do more than simply not participate. At the end of the book, the author suggests having students practice what they can say when they see someone being teased.

In a section titled "Why Speak Up?" Moss responds, "Because you can make teasing UN-cool. Most bullies tease because they want YOU to think they are cool. But teasing isn't cool. It's mean. If you don't laugh when a bully makes a joke about another kid, the joke is over. And when that happens, you've made a huge difference." Moss elaborates multiple strategies for teaching students to be powerful allies, including enlisting adult support when needed.

The Safe School Ambassadors Program[82] actively teaches students to observe and address harassment in their own schools. The program is modeled on the belief that students see, hear, and know things that adults don't—their proximity and insider status allow them to intervene in ways that adults can't or won't. The program asks, "What if a cadre of courageous, committed, and skilled students, the social leaders of your school's diverse cliques, those most likely to speak up, were preventing and stopping exclusion, teasing, bullying and other forms of violence on your campus... right now?"

Students (those with "social capital") are recruited from many different cliques and groups in the school. Once selected, students are invited to begin a dialogue about school climate and mistreatment. If they choose to participate, they are extensively trained on how to use powerful communication and intervention skills. The description on the Web site explains:

> The SSA Program model allows Ambassadors to be safe, cool, and effective. Ambassadors first intervene with their close friends and others they know well; this familiarity increases their effectiveness and reduces the risk of retaliation. Ambassadors also act in the moment, as cruelty is happening, so their impact is immediate; they don't need to wait for an appointment with a counselor or mediator.

Ambassadors keep records of their interventions, including what happened, the number of people involved (although not their names), the skills they utilized and the outcome of the intervention. They also participate in regular de-briefing meetings to sharpen their skills and deepen their commitment to the work.

Another powerful program aimed at changing school culture is the Don't Laugh at Me program, part of Operation Respect.[83] Operation Respect was founded in September 2000 by

Peter Yarrow of the folk trio Peter, Paul and Mary, to promote the infusion of character education and social and emotional learning principles into school curricula. The centerpiece of this program is the song "Don't Laugh at Me" by Steve Seskin and Allen Shamblin. The program uses music, video, and classroom activities to sensitize children to the effects of ridicule, disrespect, ostracism, and bullying, and it encourages children and their teachers to transform their classrooms and schools into "Ridicule Free Zones."

The concept of creating spaces in which cruel or unkind behavior is not allowed is different from policies of Zero Tolerance, which tend to be punitive responses to inappropriate behavior and result in student suspension and expulsion. I was struck, at a meeting of the Gay, Lesbian, and Straight Education Network (GLSEN) to hear an educator propose, instead, that we have school policies of "Zero Indifference," meaning that we will not let things go and that we will commit to responding to any behaviors that challenge the safety and well being of any member of the school community.

Children's music can be used as a powerful tool to introduce students to complex concepts about school and classroom climate and their roles in creating acceptance and safety. Phil and Hannah Hoose's song "Hey Little Ant"[84] (now a picture book that has been translated into eight languages), is a dialogue between a child and an ant. The child threatens to stomp on the ant and the ant responds, explaining to the child all the ways they are the same and the importance of considering the ant's feelings and families. In one verse, the child explains, "But all my friends squish ants each day. Squishing ants is a game we play. They're looking at me, they're listening too, they all say I should squish you." At the end of the song, the ant responds, "I can see you're big and strong. Decide for yourself what's right and wrong. If you were me and I were you, what would you want me to do?"

I have used this book with thousands of children and adults to raise issues of teasing, bullying, perspective taking, and peer pressure. At its simplest interpretation, the song calls upon each of us to consider our actions' effects and to realize that others may have very different perspectives. But I have also had teachers use the song to explore more complex issues.

For example, we have discussed how, throughout history, we have hurt (or killed or exterminated) those whom we have defined as "other," as "not like us." Often we have little or very distorted information about who they are, yet we make assumptions about them that render them unworthy or disposable in our minds. How do we find out about other people? What do we assume about them? I am reminded of the many references, after September 11, to people who "just don't value human life the way we do," a statement that always makes me respond, "And you know that how?" What do you know about the students in the special education program? In the high school across town? In the migrant camp? How will you find out?

Other teachers have used the book to explore issues of peer pressure: How do you decide what to do? When and how do you separate yourself form your peers if they are doing something you disagree with? What support do you need to make independent decisions? How does the line, "But all my friends squish ants each day" relate to other situations in which group thinking prevails, such as "We always throw rocks at the special ed bus" or "We think it's funny to stand outside the gay bar and harass the customers." Learning to take a stand for social justice in the face of peer pressure is an important discussion to have and is one that is directly related to teaching students to think critically about the effects of their decisions.

A song by Sarah Pirtle,[85] "Walls and Bridges," tells the story of a young girl who invites the "new kid," Jackie, to her house because they have discovered that they both love art. The girl's mother, however, doesn't want Jackie in her house because she is of a different race. The song talks about the shift that begins when Jackie's mother approaches the other mother and says, "Our daughters are best friends, I'd like to know you, too." The song ends: "How do you make a bridge? It's built of many days. Starts with a single step, even when you are afraid. Starts when you're speaking up, starts when you're standing tall. Build a strong bridge, my friends. No one can make you build a wall."

This song can be used to begin a discussion of how we begin to break down barriers between individuals and groups. How can you approach someone you don't know? What does it mean to become "friends"? How do we discriminate between doing something for someone and doing something with someone? How can we make sure that our efforts at connection don't become (or aren't seen as) charity rather than friendship?

The Children's Music Network[86] has an entire section of Peace Resources, songs that can be used to introduce issues of social justice, diversity, bullying, friendship, conflict resolution, and responsible citizenship into the classroom. More resources are available from Rethinking Schools, Teaching for Tolerance, and the Responsive Classroom.

One of the most engaging and age-appropriate ways to discuss issues of oppression with students relates to jokes. Many of the jokes students hear (and tell) are jokes about another group: Jews, people with AIDS, blondes, Poles, and so on. Encourage students to listen carefully to the jokes around them and to think about how these exemplify racism, sexism, homophobia, ableism, ageism, and more. Assign students to watch specific television programs and report what they see and hear. Explore the concept of humor that isn't oppressive. Are there jokes that are funny but not about "othering" or making fun of another group?

Set aside a time of day (or week) for students to share jokes that aren't oppressive, both as an opportunity to have some fun and as a way of demonstrating that ending oppressive humor doesn't have to mean that they will all be somber and unable to laugh. Create a class joke book that models non-oppressive humor.

Then, perhaps most challenging, explore with students what they can say if someone tells an inappropriate joke in front of them. Many people are reluctant to say anything because they then become the target of comments such as "Don't tell those jokes in front of Mara, she has no sense of humor." Help students develop repertoires of "What to say when..."

With older students, it is possible to explore why it is sometimes more difficult to challenge oppressive behavior when there is a power differential; telling your boss that his comment was racist may be difficult and ill advised. Such conversations can be rich and exciting for all involved, honoring the struggles we all face when we become more aware of oppression and yet often confused about what constitutes an appropriate or effective response.

STANDING OUR GROUND

We are poised at a moment of history—perhaps we always are—when there are numerous competing agendas and forces in the world. We stand at a crossroads. What kind of world do we want? What do we see as our collective future? What kind of people do we want to be surrounded by? How do we want to live with one another? A civil society demands that we embrace our interconnectedness and our responsibility for a collective future. A hole in the rowboat will sink all of us. Eugene Marcus, the man with autism whom I mentioned at the beginning of chapter 6, says: "If people are serious about wanting to live in a real democracy, then they have to run schools like schools and not like exclusive secret societies that you have to pass an initiation to join. I know nobody tried to do that, but unless membership is guaranteed, it's like everyone grew up in prep school and didn't even know it."

Do we want schools driven by test scores, with teachers and students pressured to achieve in narrowly defined areas, eliminating anyone who stands in the way? Or do we want loving learning communities in which all people feel responsible for one another, understanding of diversity, and confident of their individual and collective agency? What role will our young people play in the world we envision, and how will we help them to develop the attitudes, skills, and inclinations that will make this dream a reality?

The experiences we provide for our young people today will shape how they see themselves, one another, and the world. They will either learn to see possibility and hopefulness in the world, or they will become cynical and hardened to others' pain.

I wrote this poem for Jowonio School (a fully inclusive school) to capture the importance for the future of the lessons learned today:

What the Children of Jowonio Know

The children of Jowonio know—not because they have been told, but because they have lived it

That there is always room for everyone—in the circle and at snack time and on the playground—and even if they have to wiggle a little to get another body in and even if they have to find a new way to do it, they can figure it out—and so it might be reasonable to assume that there's enough room for everyone in the world.

The children of Jowonio know—not because they have been told, but because they have lived it

That children come in a dazzling assortment of sizes, colors and shapes, big and little and all shades of brown and beige and pink, and some walk and some use wheelchairs but everyone gets around and that same is boring—and so it might be reasonable to assume that everyone in the world could be accepted for who they are.

The children of Jowonio know—not because they have been told, but because they have lived it

That there are people who talk with their mouths and people who talk with their hands and people who talk by pointing and people who tell us all we need to know with their bodies if we only listen well—and so it might be reasonable to assume that all the people of the world could learn to talk and listen to each other.

The children of Jowonio know—not because they have been told, but because they have lived it

That we don't send people away because they're different or even because they're difficult, and that all people need support and that if people are hurting, we take the time to notice, and that words can build bridges and hugs can heal—so it might be reasonable to assume that all the people on the planet could reach out to each other and heal the wounds and make a world fit for us all.

On my wall there is a painting by Ann Altman with a quote by Diane Ackerman. It reads: "I swear I will not dishonor my soul with hatred, but offer myself humbly as a guardian of nature, as a healer of misery, as a messenger of wonder, as an architect of peace." This is my hope for all of us—that we are able to turn our loving attention to the task of creating a just society. And that we begin that task by living inclusively from the beginning and by teaching our children that, as Pete Seeger said, "Either all of us get over the rainbow . . . or none of us do."

Acknowledgments

Writing acknowledgments for a book on inclusion and widening circles is particularly challenging. I want to include everyone who has touched my life or taught me about community... and it would be an endless list. Each day, new people get added to my personal widening circles, and I am grateful to the many people who help me understand that love is not finite and that kindness is not a zero-sum game. As Malvina Reynolds said, "Love is something if you give it away, you end up having more." If I wait even one more day to write the acknowledgments, there will be four new people on my list.

Despite this wonderful challenge, I will try to acknowledge some of the many communities and people who shape my world and my vision. From all of these sources I gather glimmers and images of the world as it can be and as we can make it.

This book is dedicated to Bob Blue—educator, songwriter, child advocate, and friend. Bob listened to children as though they mattered, and because of his deep listening, he learned many things. He turned what he learned into songs and plays that have enriched the lives and nurtured the spirits of small and large humans alike. Most of all, Bob believed that people really want to be good and kind and courageous, and his deep belief in that goodness translated into a fervent commitment to making the world right for everyone. His love and inspiration will be with me forever.

The Syracuse Community Choir and its leader, Karen Mihalyi, teach me that truly, "All God's Critters Got a Place in the Choir." We live and laugh and sing inclusively, and we sound awesome because of our diversity and our connections.

The people of the Children's Music Network, the People's

Music Network, and Syracuse Cultural Workers all inspire me with hope for our collective future.

The Wild Ginger Community allows me to have sustaining experiences of community, closeness and connection, reminding me that we can support one another with love, even in times of challenge.

My association with Women Transcending Boundaries, formed after the events of September 11, 2001, has deepened my commitment to interreligious dialogue and the power of women to change the world.

As the daily news reports stories of war and catastrophe, the peace groups of which I am a member—the Syracuse Peace Council and Syracuse Jews for Peace—help me to stay grounded and hopeful.

My DansKinetics Community, led by Megha Nancy Buttenheim, and my NIA Community, led by Pam LeBlanc, fill my heart with joy and allow me to move through my world with a little more grace.

My "intentional family," with whom I have dinner every Thursday night, reminds me that we can create the community we need in our lives and that we all need people of different ages to stay alive and vibrant. To Steve Reiter, Annegret Schubert, Emmi Schubert Reiter, Andy Mager, Cheri Capparelli, Eli Marco Mager, Barb Garii, and Mayer Shevin, my eternal gratitude for our little community of love.

I am grateful to the many friends who support me and nourish me in so many ways: Sherry Chayat, Diane Swords, Peter Swords, Karen Mihalyi, Ann Goodgion, Jack Manno, Kim Rombach, Jamie King Rombach, Robin Smith, Micki Grimland, Janet Chance, and Elizabeth Stone

My professional friends and colleagues, particularly the members of the Invisible College on Social Justice Teaching, inspire me with their dedication and intelligence: Suzi SooHoo, Nancy Schniedewind, Julie Andrejewski, Saul Duarte, Norma Smith, Dolores Gaunty-Porter, Beth Blue Swadener, Lee Bell, Maurianne Adams, Robin Smith, Karen Cadiero-Kaplan.

My colleagues at Syracuse University challenge me to practice what I preach, and I am deeply appreciative of their friendship and support: Joe Shedd, Kathy Hinchman, Rachel Brown, Kristiina Montero, Jill Christian-Lynch, Julie Causton-Theoharis, George Theoharis, Jerry Mager, Carrie Jefferson Smith and Richard Breyer.

More distant colleagues also teach me so much and help me broaden my understanding: Paula Kluth, David Pitonyak, Norm Kunc, Emma Van DerKlift, and Mary Falvey.

A sincere thank you to the Fialka-Feldman Family: Janice, Rich, Micah, and Emma, and their friends Oliver Hersey, Matt Weinger, Matthew Boyd, and Jan Boyd for sharing their stories. Their living, breathing example of inclusion grounds this book in possibility.

My gratitude to all those whose stories and words appear in my head and in my text: Norm Kunc, Alfie Kohn, Jim Sinclair, Carrie Jefferson Smith, Bob Williams, David Pitonyak, Jim Sinclair, Robin Smith, John O'Brien, Mary Falvey, John Murray, Myrna Murray, Bana Najdawi, Sarah Pirtle, Jenny Heitler-Klevans, David Heitler-Klevans, Mike Stern, Phil Hoose, Charlie King, and Karen Brandow.

My thanks to Bill Ayers, who helped make the original *shiddach* for this book and who is fiercely supportive at all times.

Andy Hrycyna, my editor at Beacon, had deep faith in this book from the beginning. From our initial lunch conversation where the book was "born" until this moment, he has been an appreciative listener, a thoughtful questioner, and a consistent cheerleader. This book wouldn't have happened without him. Appreciation also to Lisa Sacks and Norma McLemore for their skills and support.

My daughters, Dalia Sapon-Shevin and Leora Sapon-Shevin, now both wonderful young women, are at the heart of this book. I am so appreciative of their willingness to let me share personal family stories with them at the center. Without their generous permission, the book would be full of holes! Dalia inspires me with her artwork and her fierce determination to make all people "visible." Leora transforms the world through her compassion for others and her great joyfulness. Their sisterly love also presents a model of how people can love and sustain one another. This book would not have happened without them.

Much love to my parents, Rhoda Sapon and Stanley Sapon, who have continued to love and support me on my life's journey, reminding me that I should keep my options open and that cooperation is always best.

My deep appreciation to Mayer Shevin, whose encyclopedic knowledge of songs and stories, deep wisdom, and kind heart always provide me with inspiration and refuge. His painstaking (but not pain-giving) editing of this manuscript was a huge contribution.

Loving gratitude to Barbara Garii, who has opened up a new corner of my heart and cheered me on as I wrote this book. Her reminders to eat, sleep, and breathe are evidence of both her deep caring and her insider knowledge of how easily I forget.

Notes

1. For the full text of Mary Falvey's keynote address on inclusion, see the Web site of the educational advocacy organization TASH (www.tash.org).
2. Vivian Paley, *You Can't Say You Can't Play,* Cambridge, Mass.: Harvard University Press, 1992.
3. For more of Bob's wonderful music, see www.bobblue.org. Also visit the Web site of the Children's Music Network (www.cmnonline.org) for more songs about courage.
4. These two organizations will be explored in more depth in Part Three.
5. For more information on the principle of tikkun olam, see www.innerfrontier.org/practices/tikkunolam.htm.
6. See Linda Davern, Mara Sapon-Shevin, Michaela D'Aquanni, Mary Fisher, Mark Larson, James Black, and Stacy Minondo, Drawing distinctions between coherent and fragmented efforts at building inclusive schools, *Equity and Excellence in Education* 30, 3 (1997): 31–39.
7. Beattie v. State Board of Education, City of Antigo, 1919.
8. For a horrifying expose of the abandonment of people with disabilities in institutions, see Burton Blatt and Fred Kaplan's *Christmas in Purgatory,* Syracuse, N.Y.: Human Policy Press, 1974.
9. For information on one-room schoolhouses, see www2.johnstown.k12 .oh.us/cornell/.
10. See, for example: A. Artilles, The dilemma difference: Enriching the disproportionality discourse with theory and context, *Journal of Special Education* 32 (1998): 25–31; A. Artilles and S. Trent, Overrepresentation of minority students in special education: A continuing debate, *Journal of Special Education* 27 (1994): 410–437; P. Bynoe, Rethinking and retooling teacher preparation to prevent perpetual failure by our children, *Journal of Special Education* 32 (1998): 37–40; J. D. Finn, Patterns in special education placement as revealed by the OCR survey, in *Placing Children in Special Education: A Strategy for Equity,* ed. K. A. Heller, W. H. Holtzman, and S. Messick, Washington, D.C.: National Academy Press, 1982, pp. 322–381; R. Gersten and J. Woodward, The language-minority student and special education: Issues, trends, and paradoxes, *Exceptional Children* 60, 4 (1984): 310–322; B. Harry, *The Disproportionate Representation of Minority Students in Special Education: Theories and Recommendations,* Alexandria, Va.: National Association of State Directors of Special Education, 1984;

D. P. Oswald, M. J. Coutinho, A. M. Best, and N. N. Singh, Ethnic representation in special education: The influence of school-related economic and demographic variables, *Journal of Special Education* 32, 3 (1999): 194–206; and J. Patton, The disproportionate representation of African Americans in special education: Looking behind the curtain for understanding and solutions, *Journal of Special Education* 32 (1998): 24–31.

11. See Steven J. Taylor, Caught in the continuum: A critical analysis of the principle of the least restrictive environment, *Journal of the Association for the Severely Handicapped* 13, 1 (spring 1988). Reprinted in *Research and Practices for Persons with Severe Disabilities* 29, 4: 218–230.

12. Lloyd Dunn, Special education for the mildly retarded: Is much of it justifiable? *Exceptional Children* 35, 1 (1968): 5–22.

13. See C. Carlberg and K. Kavale, The efficacy of special versus regular class placement for exceptional children: A meta-analysis, *Journal of Special Education* 14 (1980): 259–309; P. Hunt, L. Goetz, and J. Anderson, The quality of IEP objectives associated with placement in integrated versus segregated school sites, *Journal of the Association for Persons with Severe Handicaps* 11, 2: 125–130; P. Hunt, F. Farron-Davies, S. Beckstead, D. Curtis, and L. Goetz, Evaluating the effects of placement of students with severe disabilities in general education versus special education, *Journal of the Association for Persons with Severe Handicaps* 19, 3 (1994): 200–214; and C. Kennedy, S. Shulka, and D. Fryxell, Comparing the effects of educational placement on the social relationships of intermediate school students with severe disabilities, *Exceptional Children* 64, 1 (1997): 31–48.

14. For information on dropout rates, see National Organization on Disability (2000), 2000 N.O. D./Harris Survey of Americans with Disabilities, Washington D.C.: National Organization on Disability. Retrieved April 4, 2005, from www.nod.org/content.cfm?id=1076#educ. For information on employment rates, see J. Blackorby and M. Wagner, Longitudinal postschool outcomes of youth with disabilities: Findings from the national longitudinal transition study, *Exceptional Children* 62, 5 (1996): 399–413.

15. R. F. Schnorr, "Peter? He comes and goes. . . . First graders' perspectives on a part-time mainstream student, *Journal of the Association for Persons with Severe Handicaps* 15, 4 (1990): 231–240.

16. Doug Biklen, The myth of clinical judgment, *Journal of Social Issues* 44 (1988): 127–140.

17. Paula Kluth, Richard A. Villa, and Jacqueline S. Thousand, "'Our school doesn't offer Inclusion' and other legal blunders," *Educational Leadership* 59, 4 (December 2001/January 2002): 24–27.
18. A. Karagiannis, S. Stainback, and W. Stainback, Historical overview of inclusion, in *Inclusion: A Guide for Educators,* ed. S. Stainback and W. Stainback, Baltimore: Brookes, 1996, pp. 17–28.
19. National Council on Disability, Back to school on civil rights (NCD #00–283), Washington, D.C.: Author, January 25, 2000.
20. Kluth et al., "'Our school doesn't offer inclusion,'" p. 24.
21. From a post by Carolyn Das to the Web site of P.S. IDEA (Parents Supporting I.D.E.A.), www.psidea.org/inclusion/4.htm.
22. For those who are critical of the principles of inclusion, see L. M. Lieberman, Preserving special education for those who need it, in *Controversial Issues Confronting Special Education: Divergent Perspectives,* ed. W. Stainback and S. Stainback, Boston: Allyn and Bacon, 1995, pp. 16–27; see also, J. M. Kauffman and D. P. Hallahan, eds., *The Illusion of Full Inclusion: A Comprehensive Critique of a Current Special Education Bandwagon,* Austin, Tex.: Pro-Ed, 1995; and D. Fuchs and L. S. Fuchs, Inclusive school movement and the radicalization of special education reform, in *The Illusion of Full Inclusion: A Comprehensive Critique of a Current Special Education Bandwagon,* ed. J. M. Kauffman and D. P. Hallahan, Austin, Tex.: Pro-Ed, 1995, pp. 223–225; 232.
23. See the debate between the author and Jim Kauffman in John O'Neil, Can inclusion work? A conversation with Jim Kauffman and Mara Sapon-Shevin, *Educational Leadership* (December 1994/January 1995): 91–95.
24. Douglas Fuchs and Lynn S. Fuchs, Sometimes separate is better, *Educational Leadership* 52, 4 (December 1994/Janaury 1995): 22–26.
25. See A. Gartner and D. K. Lipsky, Beyond special education: Toward a quality system for all students, *Harvard Educational Review* 57 (1987): 367–395.
26. John Hockenberry, in a speech, "We're not there yet!—Fulfilling the civil covenant of inclusion," given at the Inclusion Imperative Conference, Syracuse University, Syracuse, New York, April 21, 2006.
27. D. Staub, E. Schwartz, C. Gallucci, and C. Peck, Four portraits of friendship at an inclusive school, *Journal of the Association for Persons with Severe Handicaps* 19, 4 (1994): 314–425; P. Hunt, M. Alwell, and F. Farron-Davis, Creating socially supportive environments for fully

included students who experience multiple disability, *Journal of the Association for Persons with Severe Handicaps* 21 (1996): 53–71.

28. M. Snell and R. Janney, *Collaborative Teaming*, Baltimore: Paul H. Brookes, 2000.

29. See Hunt, Goetz, and Anderson, The quality of IEP objectives; Hunt, Farron-Davies, et al., Evaluating the effects of placement; and Carlberg and Kavale, The efficacy of special versus regular class placement.

30. Alfie Kohn, *No Contest: The Case against Competition*, Boston: Houghton Mifflin, 1986.

31. See L. Saint-Laurent, J. Dionne, J. Giasson, E. Royer, C. Simard, and B. Pierand, Academic achievement effects of an in-class service model on students with and without disabilities, *Exceptional Children* 64 (1998): 239–253; M. N. Sharpe, J. L. York, and J. Knight, Effects of inclusion on the academic performance of classmates without disabilities, *Remedial and Special Education* 15, 5 (1994): 281–287.

32. T. M. Hollowood, C. L. Salisbury, B. Rainforth, and M. M. Palombaro, Use of instructional time in classrooms serving students with and without severe disabilities, *Exceptional Children* 61, 3 (1994): 242–253.

33. D. Biklen, C. Corigan, and D. Quick, Beyond obligation: Students' relations with each other in integrated classes, in *Beyond Separate Education: Quality Education for All*, ed. D. Lipsy and A. Gartner, Baltimore: Paul H. Brookes, 1989, pp. 207–221.

34. M. F. Giangreco, C. K. Cloninger, and V. S. Iverson, *Choosing Options and Accommodations for Children: A Guide to Educational Planning for Students with Disabilities*, 2nd ed., Baltimore: Paul H. Brookes, 1998; M. Friend and L. Cook, *Interactions: Collaboration Skills for School Professionals*. White Plains, N.Y.: Longman, 1996.

35. I tell my students that there is either one kind of learner or 45 million kinds, but not two.

36. From Jay Mathews, Special-ed fight an exercise in frustration, *Washington Post*, February 6, 2003, as excerpted at www.psidea.org/inclusion/5.htm.

37. Marcie Roth, "Don't take sides on inclusion" on the Web site of P.S. IDEA, www.psidea.org/inclusion/5.htm.

38. www.publications.parliament.uk/pa/cm200506/cmselect/cmeduski/uc478-vii/uc15302.htm.

39. A. M. Donellan, The criterion of the least dangerous assumption, *Behavioral Disorders* 9 (1984): 141–149.

40. D. Biklen, ed., *Autism and the Myth of the Person Alone*, New York: New York University Press, 2005.

41. S. Rubin, D. Biklen, C. Kasa-Hendrickson, P. Kluth, D. N. Cardinal, and A. Broderick, Independence, participation, and the meaning of intellectual ability, *Disability and Society 16* (2001): 415–429.

42. For some of the most compassionate explanations of how to support people with behavioral challenges, see the work and Web site of David Pitonyak, www.dimagine.com. See especially his article "Ten things you can do to support a person with difficult behaviors."

43. N. Kunc, The need to belong: Rediscovering Maslow's hierarchy of needs, in *Restructuring for Caring and Effective Education*, ed. R. Villa, J. Thousand, W. Stainback, and S. Stainback, Baltimore: Paul Brookes, 1992. See the Web site of Norm Kunc and Emma Van der Klift, www.normemma.com.

44. See, for example, M. Sapon-Shevin, *Playing Favorites: Gifted Education and the Disruption of Community*, Albany: SUNY Press, 1994; and M. Sapon-Shevin, Why gifted students belong in inclusive schools, *Educational Leadership 52*, 4 (1994/1995): 64–69.

45. For an extensive critique of No Child Left Behind, see Deborah Meier and George Wood, eds., *Many Children Left Behind: How the No Child Left Behind Act Is Damaging Our Children and Our Schools,* Boston: Beacon Press, 2004. For suggestions on how to push back against NCLB, see Alfie Kohn's Web site, www.alfiekohn.org and the Web site of FairTest: www.fairtest.org.

46. N. Kunc, Integration: Being realistic isn't realistic, *Canadian Journal for Exceptional Children 1*, 1 (1984). Also available on Kunc's Web site: www.normemma.com.

47. For more information on Micah, his parents, and sister and their incredible advocacy work, see www.danceofpartnership.com.

48. For more information, see the KASA Web site, www.fvkasa.org.

49. For more information on Circle of Friends, a strategy for building friendship networks for students who are marginalized or excluded, see www.inclusion.com, the Web site of the Marsha Forest Center in Canada.

50. For more information and more writing by people who communicate with facilitated communication, see the Web site of the Facilitated Communication Institute: http://suedweb.syr.edu/thefci/.

51. For more information on this research study, see M. Sapon-Shevin, A. Dobbelaere, C. Corrigan, K. Goodman, and M. Mastin, Promoting

inclusive behavior in inclusive classrooms: "You can't say you can't play," in *Making Friends: The Influences of Culture and Development,* ed. L. H. Meyer, H. S. Park, M. Grenot-Scheyer, I. S. Schwartz, and B. Harry, Baltimore: Paul H. Brookes, pp. 105–132.

52. For many more valuable resources for building peaceful, responsible classroom, see www.responsiveclassroom.org. Also see M. Sapon-Shevin, *Because We Can Change the World: A Practical Guide to Building Cooperative Inclusive Classroom Communities,* Boston: Allyn and Bacon, 1999.

53. See M. Sapon-Shevin, "Teachable Moments for Social Justice," in *Holding Values: What We Mean by Progressive Education,* ed. Brenda S. Engel and Anne C. Martine, Portsmouth, N.H.: Heinemann, 2005, pp. 93–97.

54. For resources and information about training, see www.crc-ny.org.

55. See the Web site for Jowonio School: www.jowonio.org.

56. For much more information and resources, see www.glsen.org.

57. Kevin Henkes, *Chrysanthemum,* New York: Greenwillow Books, 1991. This is one of my very favorite books for helping teachers explore the ways in which they are responsible for the social climate in their classrooms.

58. See www.devstu.org ; www.fourthr.com; www.tolerance.org.

59. Emma Van der Klift and Norman Kunc, "Benevolence, Friendship, and the Politics of Help." See their Web site for many more valuable resources: www.normemma.com/arhellbe.htm.

60. See Jim Sinclair's Web site: web.syr.edu/ffljisincla/.

61. In an article critical of inclusion, Donald Crawford (see http://my.execpc.com/fflpresswis/inclus.html) accuses inclusion advocates of having a "hidden agenda" of pushing for more progressive teaching methods. Though I would agree that this is an agenda, it is hardly hidden, and it is completely consistent with broader understandings of best practices for all.

62. See Elizabeth Cohen, *Designing Groupwork: Strategies for the Heterogeneous Classroom,* 2nd ed., New York: Teachers College Press, 1994.

63. See Elliot Aronson, *The Jigsaw Classroom.* Beverly Hills, Calif.: Sage, 1978.

64. See David Johnson and Roger Johnson, *Learning Together and Alone: Cooperative, Competitive, and Individualistic Learning,* 5th ed., Boston: Allyn and Bacon, 1998.

65. For extensive information on Howard Gardner's theories of multiple

intelligence, see his Web site: www.howardgardner.com. For more
information on multiple intelligences, see www.infed.org/thinkers/
gardner.htm.

66. See the work of Thomas Armstrong at www.thomasarmstrong.com.

67. For more information on the work of Carol Tomlinson, see her Web
site: http://www.caroltomlinson.com.

68. Pat Dukewits and Lewis Gowan, Creating successful collaborative
teams, *Journal of Staff Development* 17, 4 (1996): 12–15.

69. Julie Causton-Theoharis and Kimber Malgrem, Building bridges:
Strategies to help paraprofessionals promote peer interaction, *Teaching
Exceptional Children* 37, 6 (2005): 18–24.

70. See Nancy Schniedewind and Ellen Davidson, *Cooperative Learning,
Cooperative Lives: A Sourcebook for Learning Activities for Building a
Peaceful World,* Orlando, Fla.: Harcourt Religion Publishers, 1987.

71. James Banks, Multicultural education: Characteristics and goals, in
Multicultural Education: Issues and Perspectives, ed. James Banks and
C. M. Banks, Boston: Allyn and Bacon, 1989.

72. Christine E. Sleeter and Carl A. Grant, *Making Choices for Multicultural Education: Five Approaches to Race, Class, and Gender,* 3rd ed.,
New York: John Wiley and Sons.

73. See the Web site of Paula Kluth for the full text of an article on inclusive extracurricular activities (www.paulakluth.com).

74. See Meier and Wood, *Many Children Left Behind.*

75. Paula Kluth and Diana Straut, Standards for diverse learners, *Educational Leadership,* September 2002: 43–46.

76. A parent from northern Virginia wrote to me describing a school district so segregated that "gifted" students and "non-gifted" students
had different Girl Scout troops and attended different birthday parties,
and the parents of "gifted" students attended separate book clubs and
parent-teacher meetings.

77. See M. Sapon-Shevin, *Playing Favorites: Gifted Education and the
Disruption of Community,* Albany, N.Y.: SUNY Press, 1994.

78. See the Web site of Two of a Kind (Jenny and David Heitler-Klevans):
www.twoofakind.com.

79. See the Web site for the Southern Poverty Law Center, and then the
link to Tolerance in the News for many such articles that open up
discussions about injustice and unfairness.

80. This song was written by Mike Stern, using the words of Pastor Martin
Niemoller. See Mike's Web site (www.lapointdesign.com/mikesongs).

Charlie King and Karen Brandow modified the last verse and have also recorded this song. See their Web site (www.charlieking.org) for more songs and ordering information.

81. The DVD "...and Nobody Said Anything: Uncomfortable Conversations about Diversity" was produced by Mara Sapon-Shevin and Richard Breyer, both of Syracuse University. It is available from Teaching for Change (www.teachingforchange.org).

82. See www.safeschoolsambassadors.org for more information.

83. See www.operationrespect.org for more information.

84. See the Web site www.heylittleant.com for more information on how to use this book in the classroom. It has been translated into Korean, Japanese, German, Dutch, Italian, French, Spanish, and Hebrew.

85. For information on Sarah Pirtle's music, see her Web site: www.sarahpirtle.com.

86. See www.cmnonline.org for many wonderful musical resources to help children (and adults) explore issues of bullying, courage, friendship, and exclusion.